Students' Perspectives on Schooling

Students'
Perspectives
on Schooling

Audrey Osler

Open University Press

MT

Open University Press
McGraw-Hill Education
McGraw-Hill House
Shoppenhangers Road
Maidenhead
Berkshire
England
SL6 2QL

email: enquiries@openup.co.uk
world wide web: www.openup.co.uk

and Two Penn Plaza, New York, NY 10121-2289, USA

First published 2010

A catalogue record of this book is available from the British Library

ISBN10: 0 335 22360 5 (pb)   0 335 22359 1 (hb)
ISBN13: 978 0 335 22360 2 (pb)   978 0 335 22359 6 (hb)

Library of Congress Cataloging-in-Publication Data
CIP data has been applied for

Fictitous names of companies, products, people, characters and/or data that may be used herein (in case studies or in examples) are not intended to represent any real individual, company, product or event.

Typeset by Aptara Inc., India
Printed in the UK by Bell & Bain Ltd Glasgow

Mixed Sources
Product group from well-managed
forests and other controlled sources
www.fsc.org Cert no. TT-COC-002769
© 1996 Forest Stewardship Council

The McGraw·Hill Companies

8/12/11

About the cover picture
Killing Mockingbirds

Rough Eagles is a cornerstone project of the American Cycle, an ongoing series of classic American stories and community programmes created by the Intiman Theater in Seattle, Washington. Rough Eagles students from two very different high schools, Cleveland and Roosevelt, competitively audition to be part of each annual project (the name combines their school mascots, the Roosevelt Rough Riders and the Cleveland Eagles). The students first participate in a summer intensive, and then come together in the fall to develop and write an original play, inspired by that season's American Cycle story, which they then perform on the Intiman Theater stage. *Killing Mockingbirds: A 21st Century Field Guide*, the 2007 production, was inspired by Harper Lee's *To Kill a Mockingbird*, and explored the question of who are 'mockingbirds' – citizens who are lacking in power – in society today? The Rough Eagles created a trilogy that used elements of movement and song, commedia and political satire to tell a story about the homeless, immigrants and youth.

Contents

Acknowledgments   ix
Acronyms and abbreviations   xi

1   Making the invisible visible   1

2   Why do students' perspectives on schooling matter?   10

3   Power, representation and ethics   23

4   Researching young people's perspectives   35

5   Schools fit for children   53

6   Students and learning   76

7   Students and social justice   86

8   Children, participation and citizenship   105

9   Epilogue   133

Appendix: UN Convention on the Rights of the Child   136
References   161
Index   169

Acknowledgments

This book would not have been written without the support of many friends and colleagues.

In particular, I want to thank warmly all the students whose ideas about schooling and about wider political issues prompted me to believe that a book on students' perspectives was a worthwhile project and who took the time to work with me and other members of the research team. A warm thank you also to the local authority officers who both funded and supported the research in numerous ways, and to the school principals and teachers who enabled us to work constructively with young people in a number of schools.

I am particularly grateful for the commitment and enthusiasm shown by colleagues at the Centre for Citizenship and Human Rights Education, University of Leeds: Tasneem Ibrahim and Helen May worked directly on the project, while Michalis Kakos, Louise Williams and Julie Hastings all gave generously of their time. A number of friends in Leeds also offered warm hospitality: Hala Abuateya, Anne Gregory, Jasminka and Smail Hadžikadunić. Your support over a number of years made the impossible possible.

Special thanks go to James A. Banks for inviting me to spend time as Visiting Scholar at the Center for Multicultural Education, University of Washington, Seattle and for your generous encouragement, wisdom and kindness. Particular thanks also to Walter Parker for lively discussions, generous hospitality and for giving me the magic formula that enabled me to access local schools. My time at the University of Washington reminded me of what is important in academic life. Many other colleagues and students at the University of Washington showed warm hospitality and made my time there particularly enriching and fruitful: Cherry McGee Banks, Carol Coe, Annette Henry, Sheila Valencia and Mark Windschitl.

I would like to thank all at the Intiman Theater in Seattle who assisted me; in particular, Stephanie Coen and Leticia Lopez. I am very grateful for permission from the Intiman to use material from *Killing Mocking-birds: A 21st Century Field Guide* in Chapter 1. Special thanks also to Chris Bennion whose photograph of a scene from *Killing Mockingbirds* appears on the front cover. *Killing Mockingbirds: A 21st Century Field Guide* was developed, written and performed by Rough Eagles students from Cleveland and Roosevelt High Schools as part of the 2007 American Cycle, created and produced by the Intiman Theater in Seattle, Washington; Bartlett Sher, Artistic Director, Brian Colburn, Managing Director.

At different stages of preparing this book I was privileged to work in inspiring surroundings. My thanks to the Helen R. Whiteley Center, Friday Harbor, which provided solitude and peace, a perfect place for writing; Vicky and Winford Shearn for sea views, quiet times and good company; and Charlie Wurster and Marie Gladbach for beautiful views of Lake Washington and occasional glimpses of Mount Rainier.

I am especially appreciative of those who, during the course of writing, have, in different combinations, in the USA and at home, offered respite from the task in hand, shared meals and hospitality, advice, good music and proved wonderful walking companions: Nancy Flowers, Viv Golding and David Forster; Ellen Moore, Kathy Sorensen and Mark Ranson, and Sally Tomlinson.

My thanks, as always, to Hugh Starkey for reading the text and offering support, advice and encouragement. And to Fiona Richman at Open University Press for believing in this project and for being understanding, firm and encouraging, all in good measure.

Chapter 8 includes material that was first published in Osler, A. (2009b) Patriotism, multiculturalism and belonging: political discourse and teaching of history, *Educational Review*, 61(1): 85–100.

Thanks to Laura Lundy and to the copyright holder, the British Educational Research Association, for permission to reproduce the model shown as Figure 2.2, first published in Lundy, L. (2007) 'Voice' is not enough: conceptualizing Article 12 of the United Nations Convention on the Rights of the Child, *British Educational Research Journal* 33(6): 927–42.

Acronyms and abbreviations

BERA	British Educational Research Association
BNP	British National Party
COIC	Commission on Integration and Cohesion
CRC	United Nations Convention on the Rights of the Child 1989
ECHR	European Convention on Human Rights and Fundamental Freedoms 1950
EMA	educational maintenance allowance
ESSA	English Secondary Schools Students' Association
LGTB	Lesbian, gay, transgender and bisexual
MP	Member of Parliament
MEP	Member of the European Parliament
NCB	National Children's Bureau
NGO	non-governmental organization
NI	Northern Ireland
NICCY	Northern Ireland Commissioner for Children and Young People
NUSS	National Union of School Students
OBESSU	Organising Bureau of European School Student Unions
OFSTED	Office for Standards in Education (School inspection agency for England)
PLASC	Pupil level annual school census
UN	United Nations
UNICEF	United Nations Children's Fund
UK	United Kingdom of Great Britain and Northern Ireland
US	United States
USA	United States of America

The ethnic descriptors used in Chapters 5, 6, 7 and 8 and applied to students at school in England are those self-selected by students from a predetermined list. The list is that of the local authority in which the research took place and the categories are based on those used in the UK census. These categories, which draw on British conventions, appear inconsistent; some refer to colour, others to family country or region of origin. They have complex histories. They may be unfamiliar to many non-British readers and are often not those people freely elect for themselves. So, for example, White Black describes a person of mixed white and black (Caribbean or African) heritage. White British gives an indication of citizenship; the vast majority of those referred to as Pakistani or Indian will also have British citizenship. Race is, of course, socially constructed, as are these categories, which are subject to processes of change, external application and enforcement.

1 Making the invisible visible

Although schools are designed for children and young people, they are rarely designed in cooperation or in partnership with students. Teachers and school principals may believe they know what their students think, but this is quite likely to be impressionistic and may be over-influenced by the views of a vocal minority.

Most schools lack mechanisms that allow for the full participation of students in decision-making processes. Even when schools have active student councils or school councils, these may operate with very limited power and authority, and those students who are not members of the student council may feel their voices are not heard.

This book considers how schools might be transformed by engaging more fully with students' opinions and experiences, and by giving greater weight to their views. It examines the potential benefits to schools and to the wider community of engaging learners in democratic processes. Drawing on human rights principles, it argues that there are moral and legal, as well as pragmatic reasons, why students should be consulted about their schooling.

It does not claim that this would be a simple or straightforward process, but that it is a necessary one for the future health of democratic societies. Children and young people are regularly frustrated that their voices are not heard, and that they do not have the means of expressing their opinions about matters that are of huge importance to them in their education. Their perspectives, and consequently their needs, often remain invisible. This book is concerned with making the invisible visible. It considers questions of power and powerlessness, as experienced by children and young people in schools. It examines their participation in both schooling and in research processes, considering the degree to which these processes are both respecting of their human rights and compatible with the ethical standards applied to adult citizens.

This book aims to do three things. First, it examines a range of moral and pragmatic arguments for centrally including the perspectives of children and young people in debates about the future of education and, in particular, the everyday decisions that are made concerning the management, organization and content of schooling. It reviews and critiques claims made about student voice, and questions whether the concept of voice is adequate in enabling both children and adults to work to realize children's human rights in schools in democratic nation states, in societies characterized both by diversity and by inequalities and injustice.

Secondly, it examines schools as research sites and considers how learners' perspectives can inform our understanding of the processes of schooling and research itself. Sometimes learners' perspectives are sought as part of a process of data collection that is designed to answer research questions directly related to formal or informal learning within school. At other times, researchers want to explore complex social processes among children, as they are enacted in classrooms and playgrounds. Yet not all researchers who engage with children or young people in school are primarily interested in schooling itself. Sometimes the school is simply a site where researchers can access young people and address wider questions relating to their lives.

All these categories of research, regardless of the methods adopted, raise ethical questions about the processes of engaging with young people; about whether the notion of young people's free and informed consent to participate in research can have real meaning within the confines of the school, an institution that requires their attendance and a high degree of compliance; and about the potential benefits of the research to young people. Are intended benefits expected to be largely long term, as anticipated for future generations of students? Or should children as research subjects expect to benefit directly from the research or, at least, suffer no disruption to their learning programmes? In other words, is there any obligation on researchers working in school contexts and making demands on children's time to review their methods and establish whether there are any immediate pedagogical or other direct benefits to young people who participate in the research process?

Finally, this book reports on research on young people's views of schooling, drawing on data collected by means of a survey of all students in Year 10 (aged 14–15) in one English urban local authority. The survey data is supplemented by additional data gathered through an online discussion between students from the various schools; workshop activities with a sample of young people in two of the schools; and the collection of visual data by these same young people. Additionally, the perspectives of students attending high school in the north-west of the USA were sought; through means of workshops and focus group interviews, intended to provide comparative data.

Making sense of young people's lives

My focus for this book has developed through engaging for more than two decades in research with young people, beginning as a teacher with no research training and then moving into a university-based career. It is sometimes when we step outside our regular patterns of living and working that we gain new insights into the everyday.

In 2007, I was privileged to spend some months as a Visiting Scholar at the University of Washington's Center for Multicultural Education in Seattle. I approached my time there with huge enthusiasm, and living in this new environment made me curious about the ways in which the professional context of the University of Washington differed from the universities in which I had worked in the UK. As I travelled about Seattle, relying heavily on the public transit system, I remained in researcher mode, sensitive to the differences between the local environment and those with which I was familiar, but also to differences I observed among Seattleites, young and old, and from a range of social and cultural backgrounds.

While in Seattle I went to see a performance of *Killing Mockingbirds: A 21st Century Field Guide* at the Intiman Theater. *Killing Mockingbirds* was performed on the set of Harper Lee's *To Kill a Mockingbird*, produced as part of the Intiman Theater's five-year American Cycle, a series of classic plays designed to promote civic dialogue. A scene from the play is shown on the front cover of this book. The actors were students from two contrasting Seattle high schools; one disadvantaged and the other relatively privileged, and they were taking part in the Intiman's Rough Eagles project. The project, launched in 2003, brings together students from Cleveland, a south end high school, and Roosevelt, a north end high school, inspiring them to use the arts to break down barriers of race, class, economic disparity and physical distance.

To Kill a Mockingbird was first published in 1960 and raised issues pertinent to the civil rights era, but Harper Lee chose to set her story of racial inequalities, tensions and conflicts back in the 1930s in a fictional Southern town in Alabama, allowing this distancing in time to open up issues that were deeply uncomfortable to many of her contemporaries, which, arguably, remain difficult today. The events that unfold are seen through the eyes of a young white girl, Scout Finch, who lives with her brother and her widowed father, Atticus, a lawyer. The central event of Christopher Sergel's stage adaptation, performed at the Intiman, is Atticus's defence of Tom Robinson, a black man falsely accused of raping a white woman.

The cast of Rough Eagles was asked: 'Who do you feel are today's mockingbirds, persons who are invisible, scapegoated, or both?' *Killing Mockingbirds: A 21st Century Field Guide* is the students' response. The students' play illustrates young people's potential to make a contribution to wider debates about a range of political issues and about their own lives and schooling. The student actors worked with professional support to contribute their own ideas and perspectives through the creative processes of researching, writing and acting to create an exciting piece of drama. The resulting piece of theatre is presented as a trilogy, examining the experiences of three groups they consider to be today's mockingbirds: immigrants; the homeless; and, finally, children and young people. Throughout, the play draws on the concerns of the 12 actors, interweaving family histories, personal stories, and experiences of schooling, to highlight inequalities and injustices. *Killing Mockingbirds* mirrors some themes from Harper Lee's classic story, but the content draws directly on the young actors' own experiences in Seattle at the beginning of the twenty-first century.

Killing Mockingbirds addresses an almost bewilderingly wide range of complex and challenging political issues. The audience is required to confront a range of dimensions, moving from the family through to the global, examining inter-generational mistrust; child sexual abuse; educational inequalities; self-harm and suicide; mental illness; the outsourcing of labour; protectionist trade policies; patriotism; and xenophobia. The fast-moving script engages the emotions. One moment the audience is provoked to reconsider the meaning of patriotism by a challenging use of the phrase 'our boys in Iraq', referring to war, and used as part of an appeal to engender xenophobia; the next link to listen uncomfortably to a dialogue between a paedophile and a young girl. Satire is used to expose myths, such as those about disease-ridden immigrants.

The audience is challenged to think about what it means to be a US citizen in today's unequal world. Importantly, the audience is also asked to consider the inequalities among American citizens and to focus on those, such as the mentally ill, who are marginalized or excluded. The concerns and perspectives of the young cast are powerfully conveyed through a heady mixture of dance, movement and song; slapstick and political satire to tell a story about the homeless, immigrants and youth. These people are revealed through the play as today's mockingbirds. This book begins with a scene from *Killing Mockingbirds*.

I now invite readers to imagine they were there at the theatre. What follows is a transcript of a scene early in the play. In an epilogue to this book, I return to the play to reconsider some key ideas that have been developed.

Killing Mockingbirds

There is a full house at the Intiman Theater on this mid-week performance of *Killing Mockingbirds: A 21st Century Field Guide*. A series of pedagogical panels in the theatre foyer provides theatre-goers with information about Harper Lee and her novel, alongside episodes from the twentieth-century history of race relations in the USA. We move from the foyer to the auditorium. Many friends and family of the actors are among those in the audience. The stage set is intriguing, with red painted chairs hanging on wires above the space where the actors will appear. In my mind, the chairs hanging above the set recall the disturbing monochrome images of lynching on panels in the foyer. As I settle in my seat, I wonder how Harper Lee and other anonymous black and white children in segregated communities would have made sense of what she and they heard or saw in the American South during the 1930s.

I pass the time talking to a teenage boy next to me who has also come alone to see the play. Levels of anticipation grow as the last seats in the auditorium are taken. A few latecomers are allowed to stand; many more are turned away. The house lights go down and our eyes are drawn to the stage. We hear a conversation among a group of ornithologists. Very soon a number of colourful masked birds are flocking the stage. The dialogue is fast moving. Someone is ringing an immigrant advice line, 1-800-PILGRIM.

Recorded message

Welcome to 1-800-PILGRIM, solving your immigration challenges from Christopher Columbus to George Bush. To listen to this message in 30 other languages besides English, please press the pound sign.

> If you are calling before the discovery of electricity, please press ONE.
> If you need cheap labor, please press TWO.
> For 'coyote' referrals, please press THREE.
> If you are running for office or are in need of a slogan, please press FOUR.
> If your skin is lighter than a paper bag, press FIVE.
> If your skin is darker than a paper bag, press SIX.
> If your skin *is* the color of a paper bag – press STAR.

Call #1

Operator 1 (Honeybunch): 1-800-PILGRIM

Businessman: I'm calling from the 1850s, California. We had a gold rush here abouts and thousands of Chinamen came over to try to get rich and take money home for their struggling villages. Now there is no more gold, and there's a bunch of John Chinamen stranded out here, with no money to go home. Now, I'm a wealthy entrepreneur, and times are hard. Is there anyway I can take advantage of this situation?

Operator 1:   Glad you called, darlin' – this is a *great* time for men with vision. What you got on your hands there is a desperate and low skilled labor force – people with nothing much to lose. Have any big ideas about what you might want to accomplish? With someone else doing the work of course!

Businessman: Well, I do have this crazy dream about getting through these big Rocky Mountains and finding a way to build a transcontinental railroad ...

Operator 1:   That's perfect! Get thousands of men to chip away at that granite rock for 24/7 and soon you'll be making fists over barrels of money *and* make history!

Businessman: Well, thank you little lady. You've given me just the little push I needed. I'm beginning to see gold all around me again!

Call #2

Operator 2 (little girl): 1-800-PILGRIM

Mexican woman: *Hola* – can you hear me ... ? I'm calling from the trunk of a truck while trying to cross the border, and I don't have good reception.

Operator 2:   Ya – I can hear you. Do you have a problem I can help you with?

Mexican woman: Well, my biggest problem right now is that I don't know if I am going to make it – it's been hell to come north from Guatemala. I had to leave my five children behind, but if I didn't I can't pay for their school and they will never get ahead.

Operator 2:   Where are you going?

Mexican woman: To Washington – I heard they need help in Skagit Valley during the tulip season.

Operator 2:   That's true. Have you heard of Katrina?

Mexican woman: No, but that's a pretty name, who is she?

Operator 2:   It's not a girl, silly, it was a hurricane and whole cities in the South were destructed. They need people there real bad to re-build the cities cuz all the people who used to live there left. Maybe you should go there.

Mexican woman: Oh thank you *m'ija* that's a great idea – I am so grateful to you!

Operator 2:   Oh yea – and I am supposed to tell you too that there is a lot of work, but cuz it's like after a tragedy and there is a lot of confusion, people are getting abused really bad too.

Mexican woman: I'll have to take my chances, *ninya* – my kids are counting on me.

Call #3

Wealthy woman: Hello, 1-800-PILGRIM?

Indian Operator 3: Yes? This is 1-800-PILGRIM.

Wealthy woman: I have a very delicate situation – is this confidential? Where am I calling – you sound *very* far away?

Operator 3:   You are calling our outsourcing center in India.

Wealthy woman: India!?

Operator 3:   Yes, ma'am, you see the United States has major issues with immigration – which is kind of ironic when you think of it, because it is a nation of immigrants, but anyway, the overwhelming number of calls inspired them to contract with poor countries to save money.

Wealthy woman: Well, okay, I guess I'll give it a try; you see I am not rich but, we do pretty well. But one of the ways I hang onto my money is by hiring Hispanics to do a lot of the work around here, you know – landscaping, childcare, catering and entertaining and other odd jobs. The thing is my husband and I are against illegal immigration, but I *don't* want to lose my quality of life. What do I do?

Operator 3:	Well ma'am, I think these are your options: you need to either live up to your own principles, *or* decrease your standard of living, *or* do what many people do ....
Wealthy woman:	What's that – that sounds good; what do the rest of the people do?
Operator 3:	Ma'am, they lie to themselves. You know, pretend that the quality of life they have isn't dependent on undocumented labor.
Wealthy woman:	That's the best you got?
Operator 3:	Yes, it is for now, but keep checking back.

Call #4

Slave:	(whispering) 1-800-PILGRIM??
Urban Operator 4:	Yea – how can we help you?
Slave:	Is this safe ... ? The boss-man will kill me if he finds me.
Operator 4:	Oh sure, sure – I got you; you're not on your break – huh?
Slave:	Break? Uh ... well, I am looking for a man named John Brown – wondered if you've heard of him and if he's legit ... ?
Operator 4:	Legit? I never heard of him.
Slave:	It's – um – an underground thing – do you understand me?
Operator 4:	Oh, Oh yea – *Underground, I'm hip* – what's this Cat recorded? Who does he hang with?
Slave:	No, no – I'm the one who will hang if I'm caught trying to escape ...
Operator 4:	Escape ... ? Wait a minute, where and when are you calling from?
Slave:	It is 1859 ... I'm in Virginia.

Operator 4:   Oh *man* – you're a slave! Forced immigration . . . the African slave trade this country was built on – okay, this is a bit out of my league, I'm still pretty new.
(Presses Code Red alert).

Operator 4:   I have a Code Red here. Code Red – we have a situation here, I need back up on line #4. We have a Code *Red*!

2 Why do students' perspectives on schooling matter?

This chapter examines a range of arguments for centrally including the perspectives of children and young people in educational decision-making. I focus here on the principle of engaging with young people, exploring why children's views and perspectives should inform not just decisions that are likely to impact on their own lives, but also why their perspectives should inform wider educational policies and practices in democratic nation states, and thus be centrally incorporated into educational research, scholarship and practice relating to schools and classrooms. Later chapters look more closely at the policy benefits and at pedagogy and students' perspectives.

Across the globe, education and schooling are regularly accorded priority in government discourse and in the discourse of inter-governmental organizations. Despite this broad agreement, individual nation states accord different aspects of education a priority. Even when there is agreement over a particular focus, such as may exist in a number of nations concerning the increasing importance of international perspectives within the curriculum, in practice, different nations, education authorities, and even different schools within a nation, may vary considerably in their interpretation of this focus, with some placing emphasis on international cooperation and others on international competitiveness (Osler and Vincent, 2002; Parker, 2008; Parker and Camicia, 2009).

The United Nations (UN) millennium development goals, eight goals that UN member states have agreed to achieve by 2015, include universal primary education, alongside targets reducing extreme poverty and hunger; promoting gender equality; improving child health and reducing child mortality; improving maternal heath; fighting epidemics such as AIDS; integrating the principles of sustainable development into policies and programmes; and developing a global partnership for development. The target is to ensure that by 2015 children everywhere, boys and girls alike, will be able to complete a full course of primary schooling. The UN recognizes that the quality of education is as important as enrolment and by this it means that children who attend regularly acquire basic literacy and numeracy skills and complete their primary schooling on time. Beyond this commitment to basic skills, member states differ in their priorities about what constitutes a *quality* education, and how this quality can be achieved.

Discussions of priorities in education often focus on apparent tensions or dichotomies between, for example, flexibility and accountability; excellence and equity; and universality and diversity. How can schools develop creatively and with a degree of autonomy necessary to respond to the needs of their local communities while still remaining accountable in terms of agreed local, regional or national priorities? Is it possible to promote excellence and at the same time ensure equitable outcomes for all learners? Is it possible to guarantee universality in educational provision and rights of access to education and at the same time respond to diversity of needs among communities and individuals?

While it is axiomatic in other areas of public service provision that service users are consulted, and employers recognize the benefits of consulting with employees, education policy development and strategies for school development have rarely drawn centrally on the perspectives of learners. Parents rather than children are generally perceived to be the consumers of education, whose preferences and perspectives need to be taken into consideration in policy planning. When policy-makers in the UK exceptionally engage in consultative exercises with children and young people, these are often piecemeal efforts, which can give the impression of being little more than cosmetic. In some European countries, such as Denmark, which has a long history of democratic education, there is student representation on school boards, so enabling young people to participate in decision-making processes that affect them (Hahn, 1999; Osler and Vincent, 2002). Nevertheless, the notion that students' perspectives should be central in educational policy-making remains the exception rather than the rule. All too often parents, teachers and sometimes older students are invited to contribute on behalf of those the policies are designed to support.

In this chapter, I argue that some of the apparent tensions between goals such as excellence and equity, or flexibility and accountability, are likely to be more readily addressed when young people's perspectives are built into policy-making processes. Most importantly, I am arguing that quality education can in fact only be realized when young people's perspectives are built into these processes and when structures are put in place so that not only are young people listened to, but there is also scope for building and acting on their ideas and needs.

Education for democracy and human rights

Education for democracy is a process, just as democracy itself is a process or journey; what Dewey (1940) referred to as *creative democracy*. Dewey

([1916] 2002) makes explicit the need for the processes of education for democratic citizenship to reflect democratic principles. This was so widely recognized by the latter years of the twentieth century as to be reflected in the curriculum guidance of many national and international bodies, including that issued by ministers of education of the member states of the Council of Europe:

> Democracy is best learned in a democratic setting where participation is encouraged, where views can be expressed openly and discussed, where there is freedom of expression for pupils and teachers and where there is fairness and justice.
>
> (Council of Europe, 1985)

In the work of an international consensus panel examining education for democracy in contexts of diversity at the beginning of the twenty-first century (Banks et al., 2005), the same principle of participation is reiterated as one that should underpin any education programme: 'Students should be taught knowledge about democracy and democratic institutions and *provided opportunities to practice democracy*' (Banks *et al.*, 2005, my emphasis). Knowledge and experience of democracy are not presented as either/or. Here it is emphasized that knowledge is of equal importance to process. Learning about democracy through the formal curriculum is not prioritized over schools' duty to provide students with a democratic environment in which students can experience democracy and participation. Rather, experience of democracy needs to go hand in hand with conceptual learning and an understanding of the structures and institutions that support democracy in the wider community and society:

Yet, as a number of commentators have observed (Apple, 1993; Apple and Beane, 1999; Harber, 2002, 2008), schools remain overwhelmingly authoritarian institutions, even within democratic nation states. Figure 2.1 *Democratising the School* (adapted from Carter and Osler, 2000) proposes three pillars for a school where children's rights are protected and respected: democracy, inclusion and transparency. The processes of democratization require that teachers and other school staff, as well as students, are given real opportunities to participate in school decision-making. This requires a progressive introduction of democratic methods so that staff and students have time to work with them in an atmosphere of relative security. Yet democratic structures alone are likely to be insufficient in bringing about change.

In contexts of diversity (and I would argue that all schools and all communities are diverse, whether or not this diversity is acknowledged), democratic structures need to be matched by a commitment to and a means of ensuring the inclusion of all. This implies structures and procedures that support and monitor the participation of potentially

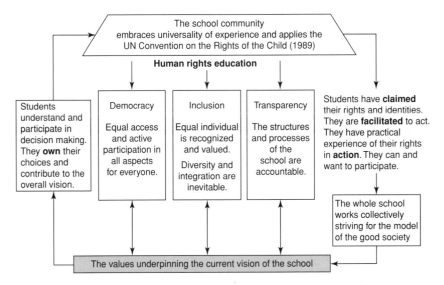

Figure 2.1 Democratizing the school
Source: Carter and Osler (2000).

marginalized groups of students, both at the point of access, and within the school. These include school funding mechanisms that ensure significant disparities between schools are addressed and admissions' procedures to ensure that students from disadvantaged or marginalized groups are able to secure school places on the basis of equality with others, as well as mechanisms to ensure that once such students are admitted to the school community, they are able to participate on the basis of equality with other students.

So, for example, in England, research has shown that publically funded secondary schools run by the Christian churches are disproportionally admitting young people from middle-class backgrounds over disadvantaged students (West and Allen, 2008). These faith schools, many of which are popular, academically successful and oversubscribed, currently reserve the right to select students on the basis of religious affiliation. In order to justify faith schools' support from public funds, there needs to be a fundamental change in the way such schools recruit their students. It has been proposed that such schools should open their doors to all regardless of religious affiliation (Berkeley, 2008). In doing so, many would be returning to the principle under which they were founded; namely, service to the community, especially to the poor and disadvantaged. Continuing access to public funds would be dependent on demonstrating admissions' procedures which support equitable access for all, and which are transparent and subject to public scrutiny.

One mechanism to enable democratic accountability among students within the school community is the school council or student council, to which students are elected by their peers, to participate in decision-making. When a school council is established, it is important that it is given real power, and the opportunity to discuss a wide range of issues pertinent to students' lives, rather than act as a symbolic or tokenistic body. This implies training for council representatives and access to a budget. Equally importantly, the establishment of a student council or student representation on a school council requires attention to be given to the means by which diverse groups of young people are enabled to participate in the council's work. The participation of both girls and boys can be achieved by ensuring that each class elects one boy and one girl as representatives, but further efforts will be required to guarantee the participation of young people with disabilities, learning difficulties, and those from a full range of social and ethnic backgrounds. In the words of the Council of Europe's curriculum guidance, referred to above, democracy is best learned in a context where there is 'fairness and justice'. A culture of fairness and justice may require more than goodwill; in many circumstances it is likely to imply critical reflection, structural change and processes of review, monitoring and evaluation.

Returning to Figure 2.1, the model proposes three pillars for the democratic school community: democracy, inclusion and transparency. Democracy implies equal access and active participation in all aspects of school life for all; teachers and students alike. This can only be achieved if the second pillar, or principle of inclusion, is operationalized: each individual needs to be recognized and valued, so that there is respect for diversity and integration of all groups into the collective life of the school. Neither democracy nor inclusion can be realized without consideration of the third pillar, that of transparency. Appropriate structures and processes need to be in place and these need to be subject to community scrutiny. Democracy, inclusion and transparency are not simply abstract concepts or principles that are reflected in organizational structures; they also become the underpinning values of the school community, which students understand and act upon.

The UN Convention on the Rights of the Child (CRC)

The principle of engaging with young people and taking their perspectives seriously in educational and other areas of decision-making is enshrined in the UN Convention on the Rights of the Child (CRC), to which governments around the world have committed themselves and which applies to all children and young people under the age of 18. The CRC operates as a binding agreement on all nation states that ratify it and its implementation by these states parties is monitored by the Committee on the Rights of the Child, a body of independent experts.

All states parties are obliged to submit regular reports to the Committee, initially two years after acceding to the Convention, and subsequently every five years. The Committee examines each report and addresses its concerns and recommendations to the state party in the form of 'concluding observations'. There are some inherent difficulties in a monitoring process that relies on self-reporting, since some states parties produce reports suggesting a degree of compliance at variance with the reality. Nevertheless, there is scope within the process for non-state actors to submit their own alternative reports, and an early report from an alliance of children's organizations presented to the Committee during its first review of levels of compliance in the UK (Lansdown and Newell, 1994) was recognized by the then chair of the Committee as representing a significant contribution to the methodology of monitoring children's rights.

All 195 UN member states have signed the Convention, although two have yet to ratify it: Somalia and the USA. The USA signed in 1995, and Somalia in 2002. Kilbourne (1998: 2) argues that the main reason the USA has not ratified the Convention is that it is perceived by vocal conservative opponents as a 'dangerous document' that threatens to undermine the authority of parents. It is opposed most strongly by conservative religious organizations, including those who advocate home education, and who argue that it would lead to unprecedented government interference in family life.

In a 'youth debate' set up during the 2008 American presidential campaign, candidates Senators McCain and Obama were asked: 'As President, would you seek the ratification of the UN Convention on the Rights of the Child?' President Obama acknowledged that it was 'embarrassing' that the USA was in the company of Somalia, 'a lawless country', in not ratifying the CRC. He promised to 'review' the CRC and 'ensure that the United States resumes its global leadership in human rights' (Obama, 2008).

The CRC is significant in that it combines political rights with social, economic and cultural rights in one international treaty. It is the most widely signed human rights instrument, having realized near universal ratification (the Appendix provides the full text of the CRC). There are five key principles that are central to the implementation and success of the CRC: the best interests of the child (Article 3); non-discrimination (Article 2); the evolving capabilities of the child/right to guidance from adults (Article 5); optimum development, including economic, social, cultural and political rights, and quality of life (Articles 4 and 6); and the right of children for their views to be given due weight, in all matters that affect them (Article 12).

Article 28 provides details of the right to education, and this right is further expanded upon in Article 29, which confirms the right to human rights education, explaining that education shall, among other things, be directed to:

> the development of respect for human rights and fundamental freedoms, and for the principles enshrined in the Charter of the United Nations; the development of respect for the child's parents, his or her own cultural identity, language and values, for the national values of the country in which the child is living, the country from which he or she may originate, and for civilizations different from his or her own; the preparation of the child for responsible life in a free society, in the spirit of understanding, peace, tolerance, equality of sexes, and friendship among all peoples, ethnic, national and religious groups and persons of indigenous origin; [and] the development of respect for the natural environment'.
>
> (CRC, 1989: Article 29)

In spelling out the right to education and to human rights education, the CRC follows the Universal Declaration of Human Rights (1948) Article 26, and other subsequent human rights instruments.

All rights are interrelated and the CRC needs to be understood as a whole. In practice, certain rights may be in tension with others, and their realization or denial may have a particular impact on other rights. In addition to the principles outlined above, there are a number of rights guaranteed by the CRC, which have a direct impact on the right to education, and on children's access to quality education, notably:

- the right to a name and nationality (Article 7);
- freedom of expression (Article 13);
- freedom of thought, conscience and religion (Article 14);
- freedom of association and peaceful assembly (Article 15);
- the right to privacy (Article 16);
- the right of access to information (Article 17);
- protection from violence, injury and abuse (Article 19);
- education and other rights of children with disabilities (Article 23);
- rights of children from ethnic, religious or linguistic minorities or of indigenous origin to enjoy their own culture, practice their religion, or use their language (Article 30);
- the right to rest and leisure (Article 31);
- the right to protection from exploitative work (Article 32).

All these rights need to be given particular consideration by policy-makers and teachers alike. The principle enshrined in Article 12, relating to the child's right for their views to be given due weight, respect and consideration, implies a cultural shift in the ways we understand childhood and in the social positioning of children. It needs further elaboration when considering why children's perspectives on schooling matter.

Article 12 and children's participation rights

Although theoretically there is no hierarchy of principles within the CRC, in reality a hierarchy may operate. So, for example, the principle of best interests of the child (Article 3) may be used as a justification for the restriction of participation rights. The best interests' principle may be used to restrict rights by certain interest groups; for example, those concerned with regulating adolescent sexuality by limiting access to sexual health services or contraceptive advice.

Participation rights in the CRC are to be found in Articles 12–17. Article 12, which relates to the child's right to have their views given due weight in matters affecting the child, is complemented by other related participation rights: enshrined in Articles 13–17. A review of the 'concluding observations' to various states parties reveals that participation rights, which are among those of greatest significance in accessing quality education, are also among those with which Committee on the Rights of the Child has struggled.

The Committee has also worked creatively to extend the effectiveness of the CRC, for example, by engaging with an active international NGO (non-governmental organization) community in consciousness-raising activities on children's rights. It also publishes its interpretation of the content of human rights provisions, known as 'general comments', on thematic issues.

Importantly, regional human rights bodies such as the European Court of Human Rights and the Inter-American Court of Human Rights have used the CRC as an interpretative tool. So, for example, the European Court of Human Rights, when ruling on the European Convention on Human Rights as it applies to the rights of young people under the age of 18, may use the CRC as a reference point.

Similarly, domestic courts may look to a body of jurisprudence that uses the CRC. This is the case, even in the UK, which is notoriously resistant to international legislation. In the case of *Mabon* v. *Mabon* (*Family Law Week*, 2005), the UK Court of Appeal ruled that three children, aged 13, 15 and 17, had the right to independent representation, in a case where decisions were being made about their future place of residence, following the separation of their parents. The Court found it unsatisfactory that they be joined as parties to be represented through a guardian and cited the UK's obligations under Article 12 of the CRC, observing that judges needed to reflect the extent to which, in the twenty-first century, there was a keener

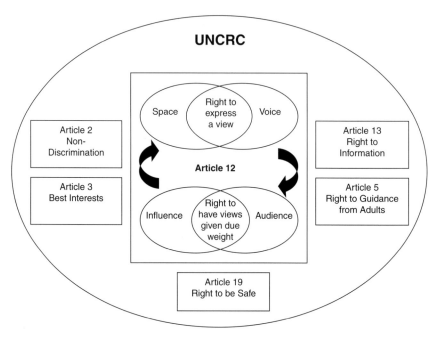

Figure 2.2 Reconceptualizing Article 12 in the UN Convention on the Rights of the Child
Source: Lundy (2007).

appreciation of the autonomy of the child and the child's consequential right to participate in decision-making processes that fundamentally affect family life. The Court declared it important to recognize that the three teenagers' right to freedom of expression and participation outweighed the paternalistic judgement of welfare.

The process of developing a body of jurisprudence that secures the principle of young people's participation rights needs to be matched by cultural change that recognizes the autonomy and competence of young people as fellow citizens. Lundy (2007) argues that Article 12 needs to be set, not only in the context of the other participation rights discussed above (Articles 13–17), and in the context of the overriding principles of non-discrimination (Article 2), best interests (Article 3), the child's evolving capabilities/right to guidance from adults (Article 5), but also the right to be safe (Article 19). She proposes a model for conceptualizing Article 12 (Figure 2.2) that encompasses space, voice, audience and influence, arguing that current conceptions of 'pupil voice' in education have the potential to diminish the impact of Article 12, since the concept of pupil voice underplays the obligation on schools and education authorities under Article 12.

It would appear that education policy-makers in the UK have failed to fully grasp the implications of the CRC, particularly in relation to children's participation rights and those enshrined in Article 12, which require that children's perspectives need to be taken seriously in schooling. In order to illustrate this point, it is helpful to consider the criticisms that have been levelled at the UK by the Committee on the Rights of the Child.

In 2008, the Committee documented its concern that in the UK 'there is no systematic awareness-raising of the Convention and that the level of knowledge about it among children, parents or professionals working with children is low' noting that 'the Committee regrets that the Convention is not part of the curriculum in schools' (Committee on the Rights of the Child, 2008: 5). The Committee called for the greater involvement of children in policy development, recommending the UK to:

> encourage the active and systematic involvement of civil society, including NGOs and associations of children, in the promotion and implementation of children's rights, including, *inter alia*, their participation in the planning stage of policies.

Referring to the principle of non-discrimination, the Committee expressed concern about 'negative public attitudes towards children, especially adolescents', which appear to exist in the UK and which 'may be often the underlying cause of further infringements of their rights' (2008: 6).

While welcoming guidelines that require local authorities to have regard to the views of young children when planning early years' services and the requirement placed on school inspectors to consult children when visiting schools and other institutional settings, as well as the duty on governing bodies in England and Wales to involve children in the development of school behaviour policies, the Committee expressed continued concern 'that there has been little progress to enshrine article 12 in education law and policy'. Additionally, the Committee noted insufficient action to ensure the rights enshrined in Article 12 to children with disabilities (2008: 7). Significantly, the Committee (2008: 2) noted that the UK had failed to fully implement its recommendations in its previous period report when it observed that 'in education, schoolchildren are not systematically consulted in matters that affect them' (Committee on the Rights of the Child, 2002, quoted in Lundy 2007: 928).

There are also significant inequalities in school achievement in the UK among those living in economic hardship. This, together with problems encountered by Traveller children enrolling in school or re-entering schools were noted as concerns by the Committee on the Rights of the Child. The Committee also expressed concern about alternative provision for Traveller children, Roma children, children with disabilities, asylum-seekers, dropouts, other non-attendees and teenage mothers. Significantly, the Committee concluded:

a) participation of children in all aspects of schooling is inadequate, since children have very few consultation rights, in particular they have no right to appeal their Exclusion or to appeal the decisions of a special educational needs tribunal;
b) the right to complain regarding educational provisions is restricted to parents, which represent a problem especially for looked after children for whom local authorities have, though mostly do not use, parental authority;
c) bullying is a serious and widespread problem, which may hinder children's attendance of school and their successful learning;
d) the number of permanent and temporary schools exclusions is still high and affects in particular children from groups which in general are low on school achievement;
e) the problem of segregation of education is still present in Northern Ireland;
f) despite the Committee's previous concluding observations, academic selection at the age of 11 continues in Northern Ireland.

(Committee on the Rights of the Child, 2008: 15)

Accordingly, the Committee made a number of recommendations to the UK government addressing, among other issues, efforts to reduce the effects of social background on school achievement; targeted investment of resources for the disadvantaged; alternative quality provision for those excluded from schools; and intensification of efforts to tackle bullying and violence in schools, 'including through teaching human rights, peace and tolerance (2008: 16). Importantly, the Committee recommends that the UK: 'strengthen children's participation in all matters of school, classroom and learning which affect them'. Additionally, it recommends that: 'children who are able to express their views have the right to appeal against their exclusion as well as the right, in particular for those in alternative care, to appeal to the special educational need tribunals'. It is clear that the international experts assessing the UK's level of compliance with the CRC are linking children's rights of access to a quality education to their rights to participate. This principle is applied both to education policy-making in general and to specific circumstances affecting individual children, including those excluded from school, those in care, and those who are subject to administrative procedures relating to special educational needs.

Why 'voice' is not enough

The *Every Child Matters* programme in England, underpinned by the Children Act 2004, addresses a wide range of services for children, including education (DCSF, undated, *Every Child Matters*). Within this programme, the British government has, as noted above, taken some steps to engage young people in consultative processes related to policy implementation. In doing so, it appears to have sought to respond to criticisms about children's participation rights, expressed by the Committee on the Rights of the Child. These efforts to consult children have not led to fundamental changes in education law, but they have helped generate debate, both among professionals and education researchers, about 'pupil voice'. The concept of pupil voice or student voice does not adequately conceptualize Article 12 of the CRC, which states:

1. States Parties shall assure to the child who is capable of forming his or her own views the right to express those views freely in all matters affecting the child, the views of the child being given due weight in accordance with the age and maturity of the child.
2. For this purpose, the child shall in particular be provided the opportunity to be heard in any judicial and administrative proceedings affecting the child, either directly, or through a representative or an appropriate body, in a manner consistent with the procedural rules of national law.

According to Article 12, a child has a number of rights, including the right to express views freely, in *all* matters affecting the child and a guarantee that these views will be given due weight. This implies some kind of policy or legal framework in which children's views are considered as a matter of course and some sort of process by which these views can be given due weight. Here Article 12 also implies not simply a legal or administrative change but also a cultural change, since there may be times and places when the child wishes to voice an opinion (e.g. in the family or in the classroom) when there is no need for administrative procedures, but simply an everyday acceptance that the child will be treated as an individual whose opinions matter in the everyday processes of decision-making.

The need for a proper framework is confirmed in the second part of the article, which requires that the child be given the opportunity not only to speak in judicial and administrative proceedings but also places an obligation on the (adult) audience to listen and to respond. There need therefore to be appropriate mechanisms to listen to children and a transparent process so that children can see that their opinions have been heard, noted and taken into consideration in the decision-making process. To be able to express an opinion, an individual needs access to information and support to express their case.

The implications are that judicial and administrative procedures need to be reformed or developed so as to allow the child opportunity, voice, influence and a hearing by an audience. In addition, the child will need access to information (CRC Article 13) and support and guidance from adults (Article 5). Cultural change implies awareness-raising and education for the public, including parents, in children's rights, appropriate training for professionals working with children, and rights education for children themselves (Article 42).

Lundy (2007) has also pointed out that children also need to know that they have the security and protection to speak freely (Article 19) and that all children can access their rights, with the principle of non-discrimination (Article 2) in operation. These last two rights were clearly of huge importance to the young people whose perspectives are discussed in Chapters 7–9 of this book. They spoke out passionately against bias and discrimination at school and about the need to feel safe and secure.

Lundy proposes a model for implementing Article 12 that goes beyond voice to encompass four key elements: space (opportunity), voice, audience and influence (see Figure 2.2). Influence relates to the concept of 'due weight' in Article 12. Children need to know that their opinions will not only be noted, but that they will have an influence on the outcome of the process. Due weight should not imply that the adults conclude that the children in question are not sufficiently mature to give informed views. Lundy also points out that the 'best interest' principle should not unduly restrict children's influence or autonomy. According to the child rights theorists she cites, children's autonomy should only be restricted when the child's preferred course of action denies the child a right to an open future (Feinberg, 1980), hinders their development (Eekelaar, 1986) or restricts their life choices in an irreparable way (Freeman, 1996).

What is clear is that, as Lundy (2007) asserts, 'voice' alone is an inadequate concept for fully realizing children's participation rights in education. An uninformed approach to student voice is unlikely to be helpful in furthering children's rights in schools. Article 12 and the child's participation rights are of considerable significance for schools and education authorities and offer not only a principle, but also a legal framework that needs to be enacted at the national level. The principle of Article 12 is also of critical importance to researchers working with children and young people. This last point is developed in Chapter 3.

3 Power, representation and ethics

During the 1970s there was a developing strand of research in Britain on student perspectives on schooling and on democratic practices in education. For example, Woods (1976, 1978, 1980) was publishing in this field and Meighan, whose main interest was democratic teaching and learning, edited a special edition of *Educational Review* on pupils' views of school. His own contribution to this collection (Meighan, 1978) entitled 'A pupil's eye view of teaching performance' examined students' views of teaching quality, looking at preparation and class management. He concluded that students' comments could be construed as helpful and sympathetic. Such work was taking place in the wake of the 1968 student revolutions in Europe and the USA, and changing public awareness of the status of young people in society.

It was in the early 1970s that the National Union of School Students (NUSS), an organization for secondary school students, was established. It campaigned for policy changes in education and in 1972 received a mention in parliament in questions to the then Secretary of State for Education and Science, Margaret Thatcher. The following exchange begins with a question from Labour MP Stanley Orme to Mrs Thatcher. He asks what communications she has received from the NUSS and receives the response: 'None'. Mr Orme continues, with additional interventions from two Conservative MPs, Robert McCrindle and John Hill.

Mr Orme:

> Is the Secretary of State aware of the legitimate aspirations of many young people to be consulted and to be treated in an adult manner in our society? Will she encourage this process with headmasters, teachers' representatives and school children, particularly as the school leaving age will be raised to 16?

Mrs Thatcher:

> I am grateful to the hon. Member for his question. Many teachers are very well aware of these facts and realise that their senior pupils should be treated as young adults rather than as young adolescents.

Mr McCrindle:

> Is my right hon. Friend the Secretary of State convinced that the student members of the union are responsible for its actions, or does she believe that others who have long since left school are directing its activities?

Mrs Thatcher:

> I have no knowledge of this particular union but I think it is important that young people at school, who are maturing rather faster than formerly, should have opportunities to express their views and should have some sense of responsibility.

> Mr Hill then asks the Secretary of State for Education and Science what public funds have been provided for the launching of the National Union of School Students.

Mrs Thatcher:

> None so far as I am aware.

Mr Hill:

> Does my right hon. Friend agree that any new organisation, if it grows, should rely on voluntary subscribed income and that insofar as any other body, for example the National Union of Students, may wish to contribute, this contribution should clearly be seen to come from its own resources and should contain no element derived or possibly derived from public funds?

Mrs Thatcher:

> It would be difficult to trace the precise source of moneys. As far as I am aware, the National Union of School Students has received to date £1,000 in assistance in kind from the National Union of Students. It would be difficult to trace any of that to public money. But I agree with the general sentiments expressed by my hon. Friend.

> (Hansard, 1972)

Questions about the power of young people in school, but also implicitly, in society, underpin the whole exchange, from Orme's introductory remarks about the 'legitimate aspirations of many young people'. Issues of power are also central to the comments about whether the NUSS should have access to public funds. The legal competence of young people of school age and their capacity to thinking independently are raised by Mr McCrindle, who implies they are vulnerable to manipulation by adults.

Throughout, it is intriguing to reflect on how young people are being represented by the different parties in this exchange: for example, Mrs Thatcher speaks approvingly of teachers treating students as young adults and states that they should have opportunities to express their views and take responsibility at school. Yet there are concerns in this discourse about the degree of responsibility young people are, in fact, likely to demonstrate. Mrs Thatcher claims to have no knowledge of the NUSS, but moments later makes it clear that she does have quite precise information on support received from the NUS. In fact, she appears to be avoiding commenting on Mr McCrindle's suggestion that NUSS members are being directed by unnamed adults.

In the 1970s, at more or less the same time that politicians expressed these concerns, educational researchers were growing interested in student perspectives. Both the parliamentary discussion and the researcher interest appear to be reactions to attempts by young people at school to assert their right to be consulted and engaged in policy and politicians.

Despite its achievement in generating debate about the position of young people at school, the NUSS did not survive for very long. It was not until the 1990s that a new organization, the English Secondary Students Association (ESSA) was established. ESSA explicitly draws on the UN Convention of the Rights of the Child Article 12 in its publicity, and appears to derive strength both from the growing international recognition of children's rights in policy and practice, following the introduction of the CRC in 1989, and from its international networking, since ESSA is affiliated to the Organising Bureau of European School Student Unions (OBESSU) (ESSA, 2009).

By the 1990s, following the ratification of the CRC by the UK government, interest in student voice in schools was growing again, as we saw in Chapter 2, among both academic researchers and teachers. There was also a growing methodological literature on research with children, yet much of this focused on research in settings other than schools. Discussion of methodological issues relating to children as social agents with rights still remains somewhat marginal within the education research community. For example, there is, within the British Educational Research Association (BERA), a special interest group on Research Methodology in Education but its aims make no direct reference to children and young people (BERA, 2009). BERA's guidelines do make reference to the CRC and require researchers to comply with its Articles 3 and 12, indicting that 'Children should therefore be facilitated to give fully informed consent' (BERA 2004: 7). Organizations such as the National Children's Bureau (NCB), which encourage research that promotes a more holistic view of children's lives, have published comprehensive and helpful guidelines on research with children (NCB, 2003).

This chapter discusses issues of power, representation and ethics in research with children. The suggestion is not that we need to develop different ethical standards when engaging with children and young people, simply because they are children, but that it is important to think through issues of power, representation and ethics as they apply to children, since children remain a marginalized group within society and common-sense views and dominant conceptions of childhood may cloud researchers' judgements when applying ethical standards to children and young people.

Issues of power and representation are central to any research agenda. As we have seen, in the introductory statements about the NUSS, issues of power, representation and student participation are not just questions relating to research agendas but are also central to children's engagement in social and political life and to debates about children's voice (Lansdown, 1995; 2001; Hallett and Prout, 2003).

Power and representation in research processes

Christensen (2004), in a discussion of ethnographic work with children, illustrated with reference to her research into children's heath and well-being, discusses three themes relating to children's participation in research: dialogic process, by which children's own experiences, interests and values interact with the research process; the distinctive role of the (adult) fieldworker; and the ways in which power is embodied in the processes of research.

She suggests that one-off research encounters with young people risk not providing a proper context in which they can respond in accordance with their own views and engage on their own terms with the research process. She recalls how although children may cooperate with the researcher, they may not see the point of the questions. She notes that even when she allowed children independence in developing the theme of a conversation within an interview and deciding when they wished the interview to stop, they later recalled the questions as silly. Consequently, through *looking* and *listening attentively* to children, she learned to imitate their own practices, so, for example, not joining in any activity until she had first observed what was going on, or until invited, just as children did. Her aim was to understand the social world of the children in order to facilitate the research process. This required her to prioritize what was going on among children and not to let herself be interrupted by adult talk, which normally takes precedence over children's talk and explanations. The children in her study were aged between 6 and 10, but her observations also raise questions about research with older students, and the ways in which education researchers interact with them.

Education researchers often face huge constraints of time and resources and may feel it is not possible to take into consideration the points raised by Christensen. Nevertheless, her arguments are persuasive and deserve consideration. The issues are important; first, because they call on re-searchers to reconsider the position of the child in research and the degree to which these relationships between the researcher and the researched are based on mutual trust, understanding and reciprocity. Equally im-portantly, they have implications for the validity of the research process and for the process of analysis. If children's or young people's view-points/perspectives are represented in such a way as to have little mean-ing for the children/young people themselves, can the research be judged authentic, informative, or even useful? In Box 3.1, I have drawn on Chris-tensen to develop a series of questions designed to encourage reflection on issues of power and representation in qualitative research with children and young people.

Values and principles

The NCB has produced a statement of values and principles, which it aims to underpin all its activities, including research. These values and principles reflect the complex ethics that apply in educational research, as in all social research. The principles reflect the fact that children are the primary focus of the NCB's interest, rather than policy-makers or service providers, including teachers and parents. NCB stresses: listening to and including the perspective of children and young people in our research; taking a holistic view of the child; and working across boundaries, between professionals, agencies, and those that exist between children and adults.

Research that includes the perspectives of children is clearly valuable to policy-makers, although it might be argued research that encompasses the perspectives of many different interest groups in a particular social context, including children, is perhaps of greatest value. While students' perspectives have often been ignored in studies of schooling and children have in many ways been treated as an invisible minority, other perspec-tives, those of professionals, parents and so on, also need to be considered in any analysis. In such an analysis is it is important to remember how children have historically been an invisible, minoritized group, and to take account of this.

While students' perspectives are critical and have often been neglected, it is important also to remember that they are likely to contain what the perspectives of any particular group contain; namely, what Kenway

Box 3.1 Power and representation in research with children: questions for reflection

Educational research processes

- What key issues of representation need to be considered?
- How is power embedded in the research process?
- What are the implications of this for preparation, interaction with children and analysis?

Preparation

- How will researchers familiarize themselves with the social worlds of the children before engaging with the substantive research issues?
- How might children be appropriately involved in the research design?
- How will researchers present the aims of the study to the children?
- Can we assume children will be interested in the research questions just because they are engaged in the education process under investigation?

Processes of interaction

- Should be researcher adopt the 'least adult role'? (Pollard and Filer, 1996; Mayall, 2000)
- Are any questions posed at the request of the participants?
- Is the research reinforcing inherent generational power relationships between children and adults?
- What techniques will encourage children's active engagement with the research issues?
- If the research design requires ongoing relationships with children how will researchers ensure that children will want these relationships to continue throughout the process?
- Do children have the right to express their views or remain silent?
- Is there reciprocity between researcher and researched?

Analysis

- How might children be involved in advice or reference groups?
- How might the analysis be tested against children's understandings?
- How will the perspectives of marginalized groups of children and young people be represented in the findings?

Outcomes

- How will the results of the research be made available to participants?
- How might the results be made available to other children?

(2003: xii) refers to as 'elements of both blindness and insight'. She continues, in reference to studies of gender and schooling:

The danger of this emphasis on listening is that it may lead to policies and practices that build on the blindnesses rather than the insights and so reinscribe traditional gender identities that are no longer viable in these times which require a certain gender fluidity and flexibility.

This is not to underplay the key importance of listening to children, who have traditionally been seen as less than competent, less than autonomous actors and consequently, less than citizens, with few rights and entitlements. Children still face tremendous hurdles in being listened to and their evidence, for example, in courts of law, is often challenged merely because they are children. Instead, I am arguing that students' understandings of schooling need to be complemented by other standpoints, including the views of the various professionals involved. This does not mean that in every study all interest groups' perspectives need to be explored. Researchers have a number of tools and sources of evidence to hand. The research literature may provide other insights, which may support, enhance or even challenge their perspectives.

We also need to be sensitive to the different perspectives of particular groupings of children, recognizing that there is not one child or student perspective, but many. So, for example, the perspectives, experiences and priorities of marginalized groups of young people, such as refugee children, are likely to be significantly different. For this reason, projects in which the young people themselves engage as researchers may play a key role in illuminating these perspectives, allowing the young people to identify the research questions and to evaluate the services on offer to them (Kirby et al., 2001).

Taking a holistic view of the child may involve research that takes place in a variety of settings, rather than one, in order to understand the child's perspectives on that one area, such as health or education. This is a particular challenge to education researchers who see children and young people first and foremost as learners, rather than people who happen to be at school. It may be important for educational researchers to remind themselves frequently of the complex, multiple and shifting identities of our research subjects, who may provide different perspectives on the same question, depending on the context in which the research is carried out.

Working across boundaries is for education researchers likely to become easier as schools and other educational institutions are also increasingly required and expected to do this. But these boundaries are not merely constructed by policy and organizational concerns. They also include disciplinary boundaries. There is much more that education researchers can do to work in interdisciplinary and transdisciplinary modes. It is not sufficient to argue that education is necessarily an interdisciplinary area of study, but to engage more actively with other disciplines, such as law and anthropology. So, for example, in subsequent chapters, this book draws on a series of legal cases intended to illustrate ways in which children's rights are enacted or denied in schools.

Some practical considerations

The NCB Guidelines on Research invites researchers to think about four key areas:

1. gaining the informed consent of children;
2. limiting the guarantees of confidentiality;
3. making payments to children;
4. monitoring the impact of the research on the children who participate.

Informed consent

Box 3.2 is a checklist adapted from the NCB guidelines to highlight the issue of informed consent, as it applies to children. In many situations, of course, researchers will have to seek the permission of gatekeepers in order to access children and young people. The guidelines remind researchers that obtaining the permission of parents or professionals does not negate the need to seek the informed consent of the children or young people themselves. Informed consent is not a once and for all agreement and research participants should have the option of withdrawing from the research at any time. This may pose considerable difficulties for researchers if, for example, they have gained the consent of a class of children to film them, but at a later stage one of the children decides to withdraw from the project. They may find that they have to let go of much valuable data. The practical challenges posed to researchers should, however, be secondary to the rights of the research participants.

Confidentiality and child protection

Part of the process of giving informed consent involves ensuring that research subjects understand guarantees of anonymity and confidentiality, and the limits to such guarantees. In a number of research contexts it may be difficult to guarantee anonymity, for example, if the research subjects are members of small groups; if they have had particular experiences that might lead them to be identified, but which are critical to understanding the research context, and so on. So, for example, in my own research on the life histories of black and minority teachers and school principals in

Box 3.2 Checklist on informed consent

Informed consent

Informed consent refers to the process of voluntarily agreeing to participate in a research project based upon complete disclosure of all relevant information and the recipient's understanding of this.

1. *Have children been given all the information about the research that they need to make a decision to participate?*
   Complete disclosure of relevant information should include:
   • what the research is about;
   • who is carrying it out;
   • who is funding the research;
   • exactly what will be asked of participants (e.g. completion of questionnaires, number of one to one interviews/discussion groups);
   • how will the information they provide be recorded (e.g. written record, audio tape, video tape etc.);
   • what will happen to the information they provide (including data protection issues);
   • what is the degree of confidentiality and anonymity afforded;
   • how the information will be used;
   • who will see the results of the study;
   • what benefits might the study have for participants and/or the wider community;
   • the right to refuse to participate without adverse consequences;
   • the right to withdraw from the research at any point without adverse consequences.
2. *Do children understand the information they have been given, in particular, how are very young children, children with learning disabilities, or children with communication problems to be informed and their consent gained?*
3. *Are children clear that they can agree or refuse to take part without any adverse consequences?*
4. *Are children clear that they can withdraw at any point without adverse consequences?*
5. *Have the researchers agreed a signal with the children to enable them to withdraw easily?*

Source: (adapted from NCB research guidelines, 2003).

Britain (Osler, 1997), carried out in the early 1990s, some of the individuals concerned had national profiles, and given that there were so few black people in senior positions in education, it was likely that some could be identified, even though efforts were made to anonymize the accounts and change names and other details. This was a problem that was discussed with the research participants themselves, who were aware in giving their consent, that absolute anonymity could not be guaranteed, and who were involved in making decisions with me about whether certain aspects of their accounts could be used.

In some research, the research respondents may wish to be identified, and again, this wish needs to be respected. If for any reason the researcher is reluctant to follow this path then this should be made clear, and a decision made by each party as to whether to proceed before the process gets under way.

Before giving their informed consent to participate in research, children should understand what the limits to confidentiality will be in cases where child protection is an issue. If the child or young person reveals something that might mean they or other children are at risk of significant harm, or if the researcher observes something that may lead to such harm, researchers have a duty to take steps to protect the child or other children. In such cases researchers need to be aware of the limits to their own competence and know when to seek advice. In research with children, these limits to confidentiality need to be made clear. Researchers will, of course, need to work within the guidelines for the funding body and their own institution, as well as meet the requirements of the law.

Incentives and rewards

Researchers sometimes offer small incentives for research participants, such as gift vouchers or sums of money. This option remains controversial for a number of reasons. On the one hand, it may seem appropriate to compensate those who provide considerable assistance. On the other hand, it may raise questions about the reliability of results, for example, by affecting the bias of a sample, or participant responses.

If, within a research project, adult participants would be compensated, then it would seem appropriate that young people might also be. The NCB suggests that in the case of children and young people, this reward would normally be in the form of a voucher, rather than cash. The NCB argues against incentives, in the sense of inducements to participate, but suggests that written information should be provided about any such reward to potential participants as a token recognition of their time and effort. Both adults and young people may be invited to join an advisory group, and this contribution may be voluntary, with expenses paid, or alternatively paid. In such cases, it would seem appropriate to treat young people in a similar way to adult members of the group.

For both adults and young people there are often indirect benefits to participating in research, which may include exposure to different people; opportunities to reflect in a systematic way on experiences; and a sense of contributing to the community. While it is perhaps important not to overplay such benefits, voluntary activities can enhance many peoples' lives. While recognizing that it may be difficult to engage some research subjects, I would argue that as long as young people are treated in similar ways to adult research subjects, forms of compensation should only be offered in situations where not to offer such rewards would be exploitative.

Monitoring the impact on the child

It is sometimes difficult to anticipate the potential impact of research on the research subject, and this is something that it may not be possible to anticipate. Researchers should therefore seek to debrief the encounter carefully, and if the research is taking place over a longer period, they should check on the impact during the process. NCB reminds researchers of their responsibility to assist participants, particularly when the participant has been discussing painful or difficult experiences. It proposes that:

> Before undertaking interviews with children, they should gather together information about suitable local sources of help and have these available. They must, however, recognise the limits of their own expertise and should resist giving advice or support beyond their area of competence.
>
> (NCB, 2003)

As an inexperienced researcher, I interviewed a young graduate in her own home about her future career choices. As the interview progressed she revealed that she had suffered physical abuse at the hands of her boyfriend, with whom she had been living. When she tried to leave him, he told her parents about the relationship, and they were now expecting her to marry the man. The parents were sitting in the next room.

I gave her advice on where she might seek support, but remained troubled over this encounter. Not only had the young woman revealed a painful experience, but the whole encounter felt like a cry for help. The research textbooks of the time suggested to me I should maintain distance. They implied I had done the wrong thing and that my own distress at hearing her story was unprofessional, as was my attempt to put her in touch with an appropriate source of help. What the experience taught me was that research subjects, regardless of their situation, are people first, and cannot be treated in a less favourable way than in other types of encounter.

This is, of course, as true of children as of any other research subject. Research needs to be approached with the highest ethical standards, ones that are compatible with the researcher's own beliefs and values. Ethics extend beyond the immediate encounter of the research, and research subjects should have a contact phone number to get in touch at a later stage, if and when they need to. In all research with children, but especially in research that is concerned with children's well-being and human rights, it is clearly important that not only the research encounter, but also the handling of data and the dissemination of research are conducted to the same standards. It is important in disseminating research results that researchers seek to work with partners who will support them in showing they have listened and responded to children. Minimally, this involves drawing attention to their needs and interests and aiming to influence policy and practice.

4 Researching young people's perspectives

This chapter discusses the processes of research into students' experiences of schooling. It begins by outlining the aims of the research and how the research team's agenda is linked to the UN Convention on the Rights of the Child (CRC) and particularly its Article 12. It discusses the meaning of student consultation and student participation in the context of the CRC before considering the specific research processes undertaken.

The research aimed to generate data that will improve our understanding of young people's perspectives on schooling and on issues important to students. It was conducted in an English Midlands urban local authority with a full cohort of Year 10 students (aged 14–15). The project was funded by the local authority and generated by a team concerned with school improvement. The local authority officers interpreted school improvement broadly, understanding it to mean more than student academic attainment; for them, school improvement included enhancing the subjective experiences of young people in the city's schools.

Local authority officers expected the project to generate:

- greater knowledge and understanding of the range of feelings students have about school issues;
- a deeper understanding of the types of issue that are more or less important to different groups of students;
- greater knowledge of the school practices that motivate or inhibit students in learning;
- critical issues that may inform younger students in the transition from primary to secondary school.

Article 12 and our research agenda

In collecting and analysing data, the research team considered the range of issues raised by students, the relative importance of these issues to different groupings of students, and the strength of feeling of students at different schools. Our planning and analysis was informed by the principles underpinning the UN Convention on the CRC (see Appendix) and particularly its Article 12, which asserts the right of children and young people who are capable of forming their own views 'to express those views freely in all matters affecting the child, the views of the child being given due weight in accordance with the age and maturity of the child' and for those views 'to be heard' by those taking decisions about the young people's education. We were aware that following concerns expressed by the Committee on the Rights of the Child (2002: 7), that in the UK 'schoolchildren are not systematically consulted in matters that affect them', relatively little effective action had been taken at a national level to secure children's participation rights in education in line with Article 12.

We particularly wished to understand how students from different ethnic groups across the city experienced school, analysing the data both by ethnicity and gender. Not only are there different educational outcomes for different groupings of young people, but these outcomes may reflect particular barriers in accessing the right to education and rights within education, particularly the right to participate in decision-making processes. The intention was to understand the subjective experiences of young people in claiming their rights.

The research team recognized that framing our research in the context of the CRC and its Article 12 might pose a series of pragmatic and ethical challenges, since neither the young people we planned to engage with, nor their teachers, operated within an educational culture in which young people's perspectives are systematically sought. As Lundy (2007) has highlighted, and as discussed in Chapter 2, realizing young people's participation rights in education implies much more than is currently expressed in the concept of pupil or student voice. It is therefore worth considering what is commonly understood by student participation and reiterating the meaning of participation within the framework of the CRC.

Student consultation, participation and student-teacher dialogue

Rudduck and McIntyre (2007), who led a UK Economic and Social Research Council-funded research programme: *Improving Learning through Consulting Pupils,* have suggested that student participation is a more limited concept than 'pupil consultation'. Their research goal was to explore the potential of consultation *in the classroom* in order to improve learning and teaching. They saw consultation as 'talking with pupils about things that matter to them in the classroom and school and that affect their learning'; consultation is something they hope will become 'an easy habit between teacher and pupil' so as to enhance learning (2007: 7).

One of the dangers of such an approach, highlighted by Fielding (2004: 205), is that student consultation defined in this way in keeping with official neo-liberal agendas can be co-opted like 'user engagement' to become little more than 'disciplinary devices aimed at increased compliance and enhanced productivity', so that 'in rearticulating the largely predictable list of what makes a good teacher, a good lesson or a good school students become unwilling agents of government control'. It is to the huge credit, creativity and leadership of Jean Rudduck (2007) that *Improving Learning through Consulting Pupils,* although framed in keeping with neo-liberal understandings of student voice, was able to include projects that promote more emancipatory understandings of young people's voices and engage with teachers in examining these understandings.

Student participation, by contrast with student consultation, is something that Rudduck and McIntyre (2007) suggest does not necessarily imply talking between teachers and students. For them, it is about involving young people at school level through their taking on various roles and responsibilities and, in the classroom, it may imply student decision-making, as young people work to understand their own learning styles and take action to support their learning. Although consulting students inevitably involves student participation, they suggest the reverse is not true. From Rudduck and McIntyre's perspective, it is possible to have student participation at school without teachers ever consulting with their students.

Just as Hillary Rodham (1973: 487) saw children's rights as a 'slogan in search of a definition', so Rudduck and McIntyre (2007) see children's participation today as a rather open-ended headline slogan without much firm substance. They do not recognize it as a central element of children's human rights. Since they see participation as linked to the citizenship education agenda, and since they seem to believe that citizenship education (in England at least) is in danger of evolving from a participatory activity-based element of the curriculum into knowledge-based formal civics courses, they suggest that commitment to children's participation is likely to fade.

Yet the concept of children's participation articulated in the CRC and interpreted by the Committee on the Rights of the Child assumes *systematic* consultation of children and young people, not just in the classroom to improve teaching and learning, as Rudduck and McIntyre (2007) propose, but including this. The CRC has helped clarify the role of children and young people as participating citizens in very distinct ways.

From the perspective of those who drafted and those who are interpreting the CRC, children and young people have the right to engage in school and in decision-making about their educational futures. Consultative processes that allow young peoples' perspectives to be expressed are important not simply so that adults can improve the services they offer to children but because children have the right to be treated as persons with agency. Children should expect information and support in contributing to decision-making; structures that enable them to put forward their views in all matters affecting them; and decision-making processes that are transparent, so they can see how their views influence these decision-making processes. In other words, at school as well as in other contexts in which young people are situated, they need to be recognized and treated as engaged and active citizens and holders of human rights.

The obligation to guarantee children their participation rights in education, as defined by the CRC, implies a wide range of obligations on the part of education authorities, teachers and schools. Not least, it implies a dialogue between teachers and students. This dialogue is central to the enactment of Article 12. Lundy's model of enacting Article 12 that addresses space and voice (the right to express a view) and influence and audience (the right for views to be given due weight) necessarily includes students' right to be consulted systematically about their learning in the way Rudduck and McIntyre (2007) propose. Within this framework, not only do students have the right to be consulted, they also have a wide range of rights in education that enable effective consultation and broader participation.

Currently, as discussed in Chapter 3, the structures and legal frameworks necessary to secure children's rights are missing from education policy. Genuine participation and the full enactment of Article 12 requires a wider range of children's human rights to be guaranteed by structures that will systematically give young people access to political processes.

Children's recognition as rights-holders and as active agents opting to express their views raises a number of issues related to children's social status in general and to the specific social context of schooling. Schools, as broadly authoritarian institutions, generally demand high levels of compliance from children. This is the case, even in contexts where schools are consciously working to educate for democracy and to develop democratic structures. School settings are inevitably ones in which there are differential power relations, not just between students and teachers, but also between children and all adults. This, as we will see, has implications for researchers working in school settings as well as for teachers working to enact children's rights at school.

Recognizing children as rights-holders challenges a fundamental premise of contemporary mass schooling. Children's right to be consulted about schooling and to participate in decision-making processes logically includes their right to *decline* to participate and to opt out of these consultative processes. The child's right to participate, as operationalized within schools, is necessarily one that brings to the fore some fundamental tensions, contradictions and ambiguities. As researchers examining children's participation rights in schools, we were aware of some of these tensions at the outset. As we progressed with the processes of re-search design, engaged with the young people who were our research sub-jects and reflected on the processes of data collection, we became increas-ing aware of the complexities and contradictions of our own position as researchers.

Research design

Those commissioning the research were concerned with consulting young people about their learning and teaching and other aspects of school life in ways Rudduck and McIntyre (2007) propose. They wished to feed back young people's opinions to school principals and teachers, so that a di-alogue about teaching and learning might take place. The research team was also concerned to develop research processes and a framework for analysis that supported and strengthened children's participation rights. We wished to assess the degree to which the young people in the city felt they had an opportunity to participate in the everyday processes of school and to increase our understanding of their hopes and expectations, as well as their concerns about school. Our goal was to interpret students' experiences through a human rights lens using the CRC as a tool.

Since the young people in our study were not necessarily familiar with children's human rights, nor with Article 12, they did not use a human rights discourse. We consequently faced a dilemma in categorizing their re-sponses for analysis. We organized their responses according to the broad types of rights codified in the CRC – protection, provision and participa-tion – but we also recognized that these various rights are interdependent and that young people's terminology does not necessarily match that of the legal experts who drafted the Convention. Nevertheless, our initial review and analysis of the data confirmed that students were, in fact, raising issues consistent with the three Ps of provision, protection and participation. As far as is possible, we use young people's own words to ar-ticulate their concerns about and their recommendations for school. The intention is that by using the words of the students themselves, our study may contribute to a better understanding of the ways that young people articulate children's rights.

The research was carried out in a series of stages. Over the two-year pe-riod of the project, some 2,000 Year 10 students, aged 14–15, participated in the research. In the first stage, students from all 13 schools across the city were invited to complete a questionnaire, administered at school level by teachers. The first part of the questionnaire comprised 38 Likert scale questions addressing the students' views about school, learning, teach-ers, friendship, personal identity and self-esteem. These questions were devised by local authority personnel and the 1,548 student responses to part one of the questionnaire were analysed by them.

The second part of the questionnaire, also devised by the local authority team, consisted of an open-ended task. At some schools this was completed at the same time as the first part; at other schools students completed it a few days later. The timings were dependent on school timetabling. This second part of the questionnaire invited students to complete the sentence: 'School would be better for me if . . . '. They were provided with two prompts; the first prompt encouraged the student to consider what they thought would make them a better student and the second to say how school might be made a more enjoyable experience.

The team from the Centre for Citizenship and Human Rights Education became involved in the project at stage two, when commissioned to analyse student responses to the open-ended task in the second part of the questionnaire and to engage in further qualitative research with students in the local authority. We developed two further stages of data collection: stage three involved an online discussion between students and stage four consisted of workshops that two members of the research team ran with students. At both stages three and four, we sought to refine our understanding of data collected at stage two. In the fourth stage of data collection, we also sought to encourage students to take on research responsibilities themselves.

Questionnaires

Ethnic categorization

In total, 1,890 students responded to the second part of the questionnaire. Drawing information from the pupil level annual school census (PLASC), which all schools in England are required to complete, we calculated that the number of students completing the open-ended question represented 66 per cent of the city's total Year 10 school population of 2,864 students. The data shows that response rates varied across the 13 participating schools, from a top rate of 80 per cent to just 49 per cent at the lower end.

One observation from the questionnaire data that was particularly striking concerned the ethnic composition of the student group participating in the research. Students were asked to self-classify using the same categories as used for PLASC in the city, of which there were 21 in total. There is a notable difference between students' self-reported ethnicity and that recorded by schools in the PLASC returns.

The data supplied by the schools for the PLASC return identifies the two largest groups as white British (39 per cent n. 1121) and Indian (37 per cent n.1066). Yet, of the 1,890 students participating in the research, just 565 (30 per cent), identify as white British and 634 (33 per cent) as Indian. It seems probable that white British students were under-represented in our study (30 per cent of respondents) in relation to their numbers across the city (39 per cent of students in this age cohort). The discrepancy can however be explained in part by the fact that the ethnic group of a number of students had not been recorded for the PLASC returns by two schools in the study.

Interestingly, 167 students or 8.8 per cent of the research sample identify as Pakistani, whereas only 66 students (2.3 per cent of the school population) are recorded as Pakistani in the PLASC data. Similarly, in the study, 138 students identify as of White Asian mixed heritage, forming 7.3 per cent of the sample, yet only 52 students (1.8 per cent of the school population) are recorded as being of mixed White Asian heritage in the PLASC data. Again, this discrepancy can be explained in part by the lack of ethnic data for some students in the school returns.

We do not know for certain how individual schools have determined how they identify and record the ethnicity of their students in the PLASC data collection. It seems likely that they relied to a greater or lesser extent on parental responses, as well as responses by students themselves. Where they have achieved close to 100 per cent returns, it is also possible that a number of students may have been classified by the school in question, where no existing self-identifying or parental data was available.

Significantly, the discrepancy also reflects the fluid nature of ethnic categorization. Some individuals, when self-classifying, may select different groupings at different times, effectively moving between ethnic groups. So a person may, for example, identify as Indian on one occasion, but as being of mixed White Asian heritage on another. Sisters and brothers may choose to classify themselves in different ways, even when they have both parents in common. Parents may classify children differently from the way they classify themselves, and one parent will not necessarily choose the same grouping for their children as the other. In interpreting information about individuals and groups, it is important to remember the fluid nature of identity, including ethnic identity, rather than assume fixed, stable or mutually impermeable categories.

Our data and the discrepancies it highlights also raise an important issue about the *use* of ethnic statistics. The broad purpose of collecting ethnic statistics is to identify gaps in provision or in student attainment, for example, which can then be addressed by a reallocation of resources. The city is recording just 1.8 per cent of students as being of mixed White Asian heritage, and 2.3 per cent as of Pakistani heritage whereas, from the evidence we have collected from young people themselves, both these groupings appear to be much larger, estimated at around 7.3 per cent and 8.8 per cent, respectively. If there is such a significant difference between perceived numbers and actual numbers of self-identifying students, then this raises important concerns about equitable resource allocation to meet the specific needs of these hidden minorities.

Interpreting the questionnaire data

Interpreting students' comments to open-ended questions at the end of a questionnaire poses a number of challenges. We were not aware of the conditions under which the students had completed the questionnaires, since they were administered by teachers, nor how these conditions might have varied from school to school, or indeed between different sets of students in the same school. In some circumstances, some students may not have had time to answer as they might have wished, given that the open-ended questions were completed on a subsequent occasion. Some students' answers may have been influenced by part one of the questionnaire, whereas others may have treated the two elements independently. Some students may have had a chance to confer with their peers; others are likely to have completed the questionnaire under examination-type conditions.

Setting aside these problems, the open-ended answers were an important source of data to us, since they had been completed by a substantial number of students, 1,890 in total. The vast majority of responses indicated that the questions had been answered seriously and thoughtfully.

All data sources have their strengths and limitations. In this case we were able to amass data from questionnaires, online discussions and workshops. These different sources complement each other and we are thus able to check the validity and reliability of data for checking these different sets of data against each other. Importantly, in a study addressing student participation and rights, different stages of the research raise different questions about the ethics of the research, teachers and local authority officers as gatekeepers, and students' informed consent to participate in the research project.

Online discussion

In the third stage of the research, students from across the city's schools were invited to participate in an online discussion. This invitation to students was mediated by school administrators and teachers; three schools agreed to give this option to students. In this part of the research process, as in the student workshops that followed, teachers acted as gatekeepers between us, the researchers, and the students who took part, our research subjects. The ways in which gatekeepers may alter the dynamics of the relationship between researchers and students as research subjects is discussed below, in relation to the student workshops.

Drawing on our preliminary analysis of results from the questionnaire, we gave students a series of questions to stimulate debate. Table 4.1 shows the topics selected. Young people from all three schools took part. Although individuals could contribute online without being identified by their peers, they were required to register with their schools in order to access the discussion group. Two or three new topics were posted every 24 hours over a period of days.

We hoped through this process, first, to encourage students to contribute by using technology and a format with which they would be comfortable and familiar. Second, we hoped this process might also help clarify which of the students' concerns and proposals arose out of practices in some schools, and which were more broadly relevant to schools across the city and beyond. Finally, we also hoped the data generated would help us refine our understanding of the issues the wider cohort of students had raised. It would serve as a check to validate or possibly challenge our preliminary analysis. The online discussion also served as a form of consultation with students. We hoped students would reflect on our preliminary findings and engage in problem-solving with their peers from other schools.

Most discussion topics were introduced with a statement, followed by one or more questions. Generally, the topic was drawn directly from the open-ended responses of the questionnaire, and was an issue about which a significant number of students had written. This was the case for topics A – I. Topics J and K on 'your ideal school' and 'advice to Year 6' were designed to encourage discussion about any additional issues that students wished to raise. The advice to Year 6 topic was specifically to support the development of a booklet for Year 6 students who were in the process of preparing for secondary school, something that the project funders required as a project outcome.

Although the discussion site made it explicit that participants' messages were to be read by researchers, and that a member of the research team was posting discussion starting points to stimulate debate, on reflection, it would seem there was no adequate way of assessing the degree to which the young people who posted messages to each other were, in fact, giving their *informed* consent to participate in the research. Since the research data was collected, it has become apparent that many young people feel so safe online that they take risks, which they would not necessarily take in other interactions. Although this was a password-protected site, and there is no evidence of any risky behaviour by participants (such as

Table 4.1 Online discussion topics generated by students' questionnaire responses

	Topic	Stimulus for debate
A	Rules	School rules and class rules need to be negotiated with students. If students help draw up the rules they are more likely to keep them. Schools where students are properly involved in decision-making are almost non-existent. How does your school measure up? What good ideas have you got?
B	The school day	The school day should be flexible, so that if a student wants to make a later start and work on into the evening they can do so. Would this arrangement appeal to you? What are its strengths and weaknesses?
C	Interesting lessons	Many students believe that lessons could be made more interesting. What learning methods work for you? Is the curriculum relevant?
D	A fair environment	Schools could do more to make sure that everyone can learn in an environment free from violence, bullying, racism and sexism. Our survey showed that girls feel more strongly about these issues than boys. What are your ideas for helping students and teachers to achieve a fair environment?
E	Safety	Not all schools are safe learning environments for all students. Some students will always be vulnerable to bullying. Girls and boys have very different experiences of bullying. What can schools, teachers and students do about this?
F	Respect	Relationships between teachers and students based on mutual respect are essential for academic success. Students need more encouragement. Many teachers try to dictate to students. How could teachers and students cooperate more?
G	Student involvement and participation	A good student does not simply focus on school work but makes a wider contribution to the school community by getting involved with projects designed to improve things. However, many students told us that school councils need to be more effective. What are your views?
H	Extending learning	Schools are too inward-looking. They need to be open to adults as well as children. Young people need opportunities to study through visits, work experience placements and projects. How can schools improve in this area?
I	Cultural diversity	Schools should cater for the cultural diversity of students and teachers. Does your school make special provision for students from different ethnic or religious groups? For example, give religious holidays, consider food requirements or religious commitments?
J	Your ideal school	If you could design your ideal school, what would be its most important features?
K	Advice to Year 6	What advice would you give to a Year 6 student about getting along with teachers and students? How can a Year 6 student increase their chances of success at secondary school?

revealing sensitive information about themselves), the ethics of using an online discussion as a data source need further consideration and investigation. So, for example, it may have been helpful to have asked the participants, following the discussion, to reflect on the process with us.

Student workshops

The fourth and final stage of data collection consisted of workshops with students, including the engagement of workshop participants in carrying out research in their own schools. In line with our commitment to research that enables young people to help shape research processes and collect and analyse data, we planned the workshops so that students might receive some basic training in the practicalities and ethics of data collection; collect data; engage in some preliminary analysis; and present their result to members of the university research team.

Gatekeepers

To this end, we organized workshops with small groups of students. The workshops took place in the following school year, two terms after the initial questionnaire was administered, and were conducted with students in two of the participating schools, Green Lane Community College and Long Meadow School. At both schools we requested the opportunity to work with a group of Year 10 students, both boys and girls, with a range of academic attainment, whose ethnic backgrounds broadly reflected the school population.

At Green Lane Community College we were given a group of Year 10 students as requested, but on arrival at Long Meadow School, we found the liaison teacher had gathered together a mixed age group, 12–16, drawn from the school council's executive group. The students at Long Meadow knew each other very well, having worked together over a period, whereas at Green Lane Community College most but not all of the students were previously known to each other.

In school settings there is often more than one gatekeeper: there are various rings of gatekeepers with whom researchers have to negotiate. The sets of gatekeepers operate like those who used to guard the entrances to medieval castles: researchers must pass through the outer gates before accessing further concentric circles of the castle's defences. At the outer gate, researchers may first need to secure the support of influential people in the local authority, who will approach the school principals, to gain their support. While this is happening, researchers may have little space for manoeuvre, waiting between the outer defences and a second wall, as negotiations take place outside of their hearing, rather than with them. Once through a middle wall and into the schools, the school principals are likely to have to talk to various colleagues, and again there is a wait while others pursue negotiations. At this stage the researchers may have very little idea of what is going on: usually practical arrangements are being discussed.

At different stages, researchers may be asked to produce documentation about the project and/or proof that they have been security-checked to work with children. Different sets of gatekeepers may ask again for the same information and checks on credentials. Finally, the researchers are put in touch with teachers who are asked to organize the visits, and they may have very little idea of the focus of the research or specific requests made.

Gatekeepers do not simply provide access. In all qualitative research with students in school settings, teachers exercise power in a number of ways. Teachers and schools can influence the research process itself, shaping the context of the research encounter and, as in this case, directly affecting the design of the research by changing the focus. So, at Long Meadow School, we found ourselves working with a mixed group of 11–16-year-olds, instead of 14–15-year-olds.

Researchers need to be mindful of the power relations between the teacher–gatekeeper and the students they hope will be their research subjects. At Long Meadow School we were aware that the school council executive members, who formed our research group, were regularly employed in the community as ambassadors for the school. At most schools, through direct instruction or more subtle approaches, it is likely that students will be reminded to act as welcoming hosts to the research team, and promote a good image of the school.

Informed consent

At both schools we renegotiated access with the students themselves, explaining that we were conducting research into students' experiences of school; that we had surveyed the previous Year 10 across the city; and that that we now needed genuine volunteers who would be prepared to work with us in two workshops, and carry out some tasks in between our visits. We promised students that their identities would be disguised and that the real name of their school would not appear in our reports. As well as promising anonymity, we also requested that students respected the confidentiality of the group and did not discuss the specific contribution of fellow participants with other students. We explained that although we would offer general feedback to the school on the workshop outcomes, we would also respect students' confidentiality and anonymity. A total of

21 students decided to take part in the workshops, and just one student withdrew. The workshops lasted for one hour each, but in each case they were followed by a break and a number of students remained to chat or to complete or perfect a task.

At Green Lane Community College we immediately encountered a problem with confidentiality and anonymity at the end of the second workshop when the liaison teacher returned as we were packing away, and started to leaf through the students' work. Although we were quickly able to intervene and explain the guarantees of confidentiality we had made, this action by the teacher is illustrative of the power relations between teachers and students in many schools, where there is at best, a weak notion of students' right to privacy or property, and where students' work is often deemed the property of the school.

Researchers working with children and young people in school settings have tended to interpret 'informed consent' as securing the agreement of parents, teachers and/or education authorities, although some provide children and young people with information leaflets, verbal explanations and presentations to a class group so that individuals also have the opportunity to opt in/opt out (Morrow, 2001).

In this research, the school authorities took the decision that the young people we wished to engage in this research were competent in understanding the issues and in taking a decision whether or not to participate in keeping with their own best interests (Alderson and Goodwin, 1993) and so their parents' permission was not sought. As Alderson and Goodwin (1993) have observed in relation to research on children's consent to surgery, there are numerous contradictions within concepts of children's competence related to adult (health care workers', parents' and carers') judgements about children's ability to take autonomous decisions.

A landmark case relating to young people's access to contraceptive advice under the age of 16 ruled that in English law a competent child is one who 'achieves a sufficient understanding and intelligence to enable him or her to understand fully what is proposed' and also has 'sufficient discretion to enable him or her to make a wise choice in his or her own interests' (Gillick, 1985: 425). Victoria Gillick sought to prevent a health authority from providing contraceptive advice to a young girl without her involving parents. In 1985, the House of Lords ruled that girls under the age of 16 could be competent, and in such cases it should be the young person's choice as to whether or not to involve parents.

Of course, the school setting means that young people of the same age range but different levels of emotional maturity are grouped together. Researchers investigating children's understandings of parental involvement in education found that while students in secondary school were considered by their teachers to be autonomous individuals, capable of giving their own consent to research, the same judgements were generally not made about children under the age of 11 in primary schools. They observe: 'Age is thus an issue here, with young people being regarded by their educational gatekeepers as having the competence to make an autonomous decision about participation in ways that children were not (David et al., 2001: 361).

Yet if we examine the issue in the context of children's rights, considering both English law and in the framework of the CRC, it is clear that judgements cannot be made merely on an age basis, since many young children are likely to have the understanding and wisdom to make their own choices. This implies a degree of experience in the area under consideration. Indeed, many 9-year-olds might be judged to have equal understanding, judgement and experience to many adults. So, for example, children making decisions about their own health care will have a unique experience of the illness in question. The ways in which we arrive at judgements about children's competence and autonomy raise fundamental questions about how society recognizes children as a class. It appears that the ways in which society constructs childhood may be clouding debates about the autonomy of children and young people.

A further complexity concerns whether the provision of facts and information are sufficient for research participants in a school setting to give consent freely, or whether they may be pressured to do so, by the expectations of teachers or, indeed, their peers. Researchers studying children and young people's perceptions of parental involvement in school (David et al., 2001) concluded that their very attempts to present information to a whole class, with the intention of maximizing choices about participation and non-participation in the research project, meant that the introduction to the project was presented as part of the regular curriculum, where there is generally no choice but to comply. In this context, they suggest, they may have inadvertently made it more difficult for students to opt out.

Workshop schools

Green Lane Community College serves students aged 11–19 and attracts students from the immediate neighbourhood and beyond. It is situated in a suburb with low-density housing near to the city boundary. Over 60 per cent of the school population is of Indian heritage; some 30 per cent are White British, with a wide range of other ethnic groups represented. According to the school's 2005 Office for Standards in Education (OFSTED) inspection report, Green Lane Community College is popular with parents and oversubscribed. OFSTED reports very favourably on student–teacher relationships and notes the examination results for the school are broadly in line with the national average. Although the majority of students are bilingual, very few are at an early stage of learning English. The school includes some middle-class students, but Green Lane is largely working class in its make up, and OFSTED describes the school population as 'relatively deprived'.

Long Meadow School serves students aged 11–16 years and is also situated on the outskirts of the city. The 2005 OFSTED inspection report identified a very high proportion of the school population, some 90 per cent, as bilingual. Around 90 per cent of students are part of the Indian diaspora, with many families who migrated to Britain in the 1970s as refugees from East Africa, where they had been settled for a generation or more. The proportion with special educational needs is broadly in line with the national average. Just 6 per cent identify as White British.

OFSTED praises the school for the quality of its teaching and commended the excellent citizenship programme and the school's commitment to students' spiritual, moral, social and cultural development. Although students enter the school with below-average attainment, the school closes this gap, and students go on to achieve above-average examination results at age 16. Community links are described as 'excellent' and the school ethos is said to be one that 'reflects care, support and racial harmony'. The school draws most of its students from the immediate neighbourhood, and many of the students' parents and grandparents also attended Long Meadow School.

Workshop design

In both schools, the workshops took place in the school library, and were conducted without a teacher present, although in one case a library assistant was present in an adjoining area. The students were released from their classes but the choice of venue, away from a regular classroom, was intended to promote a different type of activity from regular lessons. We began the first workshop with introductions before outlining the research that had already taken place. We explained the overall aims of the project, stressing our need to deepen our understanding of what students believe will both enhance their learning and enable school to be a more enjoyable experience. Since the research process required data collection in school, we discussed the ethics of collecting data, and asked them to secure the agreement of individual teachers when engaging in data collection in classrooms. We had prepared a brief written project outline, which they could show to teachers, as necessary. We recognized that in inviting students to act as researchers, they too might encounter powerful gatekeepers within their own schools. One member of our research team took the lead in facilitating the student workshop, while the second took notes.

The first activity involved paired introductions: the students each introduced themselves to a partner, aiming where possible to say something about themselves that might be new to the rest of the groups in cases where they were already well known to the others. Based on what they had learned, each person then introduced their partner to the researchers and the rest of the group.

The second activity was a group discussion where three broad questions were discussed. These questions were drawn from students' responses across the city to the final open-ended question at the end of the questionnaires:

- How can schools develop so that everyone can learn in an environment free from bullying, violence, racism and sexism?
- Our city is culturally diverse. What steps do schools need to take to ensure that girls and boys from different backgrounds are treated fairly?
- Our survey suggested that students are concerned that they are not being listened to at school and are not always respected by teachers. What practical improvements can you suggest to address this problem?

To close the first workshop, we undertook some preliminary work to prepare for the task that students would carry out before the next workshop. We asked the students to imagine that they were photo journalists who wanted to follow up our research with an article on the experiences of students in the city's schools by producing a photo essay. We chose the profession of journalist on the assumption that all students would have direct, first-hand experience of the outcomes of journalists' work, but not necessarily of researchers. Later in the workshop we discussed similarities and differences between journalists and researchers.

We examined a range of ethical and practical concerns, pointing out that in many of the circumstances there were not always clear-cut answers or rules that could be applied. Students discussed what lines of enquiry they might follow and what issues they would need to take into consideration to ensure that their pictures and any accompanying text was fair and balanced. What evidence would they look for? Were there individuals whose permission needed to be sought before photos were taken? Would it be appropriate to take photos in the classroom and, if so, did they need the prior permission of the teacher? How would their photography be explained to fellow students and what could they do to ensure that their work did not disrupt the regular work of teachers or students, or cause them to behave differently from normal? Were there any places or circumstances where it would not be appropriate to take photos at all? If it was not possible to get a photo to illustrate a particular issue, would it be appropriate to set a photo up? What were the problems with this? From this they drew up a set of draft guidelines for a photo journalist that was then confirmed in negotiation with the university researchers.

We then issued each student with a disposable camera and invited them to research and take photos over the period of a week as if they were the photo journalist. The photos should illustrate positive and negative aspects of school from their perspective. We briefly discussed questions of power and responsibility given that the students were working in their own school, and needed the cooperation of both teachers and fellow students in order to carry out their work. We made practical arrangements to collect the cameras a week later and promised the students that they would be given two copies of each photo; one to keep and a second to use in the following workshop two weeks later.

In the second workshop students were given two copies of their own developed photos; the first copy was for them to keep and the second to use in the subsequent activity. They were then asked to produce two posters; one that illustrated positive aspects of school and the second that illustrated negative aspects or experiences. They were asked to provide captions and, where appropriate, commentaries to their photos. At Long Meadow School students worked individually on this task, but at Green Lane Community College they chose to work cooperatively, in pairs or small groups.

When the posters were complete, the students were invited to present their posters to the group and to answer questions from their peers and from the researchers about the data they presented. The second workshop finished with a brief oral evaluation of the process, and students were invited to comment whether the workshops or the photography had influenced their views or actions.

In many ways, the workshop activities, drawing on visual evidence and using students as researchers, resembled a regular pedagogical activity. I first used a similar technique with young people for research on citizenship education (published as Osler and Starkey 2003) and have since adapted it and run different workshops in the UK, in South Africa and in the USA, to get young people aged 9–19 to engage with research processes. The goal is to find alternative ways for young people to express themselves other than merely talking or drawing. Research workshops are intended to be fun and a learning experience.

In some ways such research workshops overcome some practical problems of conducting research in a school setting, since many young people are enthusiastic about joining in; they are learning new skills and gaining new experiences, and this justifies the workshop to teachers. Working with young people in school and withdrawing them from regular lessons can raise ethical issues as to whether this is a good use of their time. The aim is that the pedagogical benefits should outweigh any extra effort students have to put in to make up for missed lessons. One challenge to this position concerns the degree to which students see their visitors as additional teachers, and consequently view what happens in the workshop as an alternative part of the curriculum and therefore something that brings with it a degree of hidden coercion.

Conclusion

This chapter has considered the aims and processes of research that sought to generate data on young people's perspectives on schooling. Not only was the research concerned with young people's participation in their own education and with consulting students about school practices, but it was also designed, as far as was practicable, so as to actively involve the students in research processes. Accordingly, as well as responding to questionnaires, a number of students took part in online discussions and in their own data collection and analysis, helping to shape the ongoing research agenda in ways that sought to reflect the principle of participation underpinning the CRC. Innovation in data collection and data analysis, working with students, rather than viewing them as research subjects or data sources, brings new challenges and a new range of ethnical issues. It is a reminder to us that research is a complex set of processes that can often be messy. Researching children's rights, and indeed all research involving children, necessarily involves giving special consideration to children's rights within the research project.

5 Schools fit for children

This chapter focuses on students' perceptions of the conditions in which they are asked to study. As discussed in Chapter 4, 1,890 students in a multicultural city in the English Midlands responded to a survey about their schooling, and this data source was complemented by workshops and an online discussion with smaller numbers of young people. The student survey across all of the city's 13 secondary schools was described by local authority officers as 'one of the most widespread studies into the attitudes of school pupils... for several years'. It was also the first city-wide piece of research on young people's perspectives that included information on the students' gender and ethnicity.

Students in our study draw on their experiences and perceptions of schooling in and beyond the classroom. Our study centrally addresses students' perceptions of classroom learning, but extends its focus *beyond the classroom*, largely because students themselves made links between their learning and the wider school environment. These young people argue that if the broad conditions of schooling are not right, this causes tensions between teachers and learners as well as discomfort among learners. Given the emphasis that students place on these conditions of schooling, this chapter focuses on the broad context of learning and subsequent chapters address learning and teaching, and student participation and citizenship. The analysis examines student perceptions through a children's rights lens using the categories of provision, protection and participation.

Chapter 6 then looks directly at the classroom, and on what students say about the ways in which they learn including teaching styles, their own behaviour and that of others, and relationships with teachers. It is primarily concerned with rights of provision and participation, although it also addresses protection rights.

Chapter 7 reports on schooling, social justice and the ways in which young people suggest that inequalities and injustices at school hinder academic learning. It reflects on student understandings of discrimination, racism, sexism and other inequalities. It is concerned with students' participation and protection, although the provision of appropriate structures to ensure participation and appropriate education to promote social justice are discussed.

Chapter 8 takes a closer look at relationships between teachers and students in schools, as understood by young people. It reflects on ways in which school organizational structures support young people as autonomous individuals and the ways in which they inhibit individual development, cooperation and democratic participation. It seeks to extend these ideas beyond the school and addresses young people's understandings of themselves as citizens in their city or neighbourhood, their country and the wider world.

This chapter considers whether schools are, in fact, fit for children and fit for the purpose of young people's learning. It reports on how the young people in the study perceive the physical environment of the school; its organizational features; for example, the length of the school day, school rules, and the facilities and activities offered beyond the classroom. It discusses students' perceptions of the ways in which the broader school environment, physical and organizational, impacts upon their attitudes to school, and their ability to learn. Although many young people focus in on the particular details of school life that affect their learning, a minority indicate that they have a good understanding of broader issues relating to the politics and economics of education policy, such as competition for scarce resources, as it impacts on their schooling.

Research context

The research aimed to generate a better understanding of the issues that are important to students in a culturally diverse city in the English Midlands. Although the city where these young people live is multicultural, 80 per cent of its schools are classified as 'monocultural'. National guidelines classify a school as monocultural when more than 80 per cent of students are recorded as coming from one ethnic group. This city-wide profile suggests that a number of young people, particularly from within white British and Indian heritage families (the two largest ethnic groups within the city) who are being educated in such schools, will have limited opportunities to engage with students from other ethnic backgrounds.

The students were aged 14–15 and were in Year 10, the penultimate year of compulsory schooling. Some of their schools catered for young people aged 11–16, whereas others served young people aged 11–19. Regardless of the age range of the school they attend, most students would expect to continue their education and/or training through to the age of 18, and many would hope to continue after that to university. A full account of the research methods, including the survey, workshop and online discussion is provided in Chapter 4.

We collected data on the gender and ethnicity of students who took part in the survey and we also invited the young people who took part in the workshops to provide self-descriptions. Typically these descriptions made reference to gender with around half of the students also describing themselves with reference to their religion. Around one in four made reference to ethnicity. Some self-descriptions also include information about the individual's ambitions or personality and may make reference to their family. So, for example, Selma's self descriptor reads: 'Female, European Muslim'; Jade's reads: 'Christian, half Caribbean, half white'; Hamzalah describes himself as: 'Male, Muslim, funny, sarcastic'; Katie's contains no information on ethnicity or religion: 'I am a teenage female and I am very easy going, helpful and comical'; and Kirandeep describes herself as 'Female, Sikh, easy-going, unique, ambitious'.

What is notable is that as in other studies (Osler and Starkey, 2003; Hill et al., 2007), young white people from the majority population tend to avoid any reference to ethnicity. White as a category remains an uncomfortable one for many white people, and for many scholars (particularly white scholars) who recognize in ethnic categorization the dangers of homogenizing white people (Hill et al., 2007) in ways not all of them would recognize when using terms such as 'ethnic minority' or 'black and minority ethnic'. By collecting information on the ethnicity of those surveyed and by inviting young people in workshops to self-identify in the ways described above, we have collected data that allows us to consider differences in the ways that young people experience school according to gender and ethnicity. The study differs in this respect from other studies of student consultation and student voice.

Like us, Arnot and Raey (2004) set out to consider the perspectives of students who differed by class, gender and ethnicity in, in their case, two contrasting schools with different pedagogic traditions. They found the students in their study emphasized gender, 'ability' and classroom behaviour as aspects of their identities that influence conditions of learning. Consequently, it is these factors on which the researchers choose to focus.

Competing voices?

Rudduck and McIntyre (2007: 162, original emphasis) in their report of the ESRC funded project *Improving Learning through Consulting Pupils* note that:

> one of the strengths of discussing teaching and learning [with pupils] is that it provides the opportunity for pupils to see that different individuals or sub-groups in their class *may* have different experiences of the same situation and different views on how their learning can be improved.

They draw on the work of Stewart Ranson (2000: 65) who argues the need to 'reconstruct a theory of citizenship' that is 'grounded in the experience of homogeneity' and, importantly, allows different groups 'to enter a discourse in which they voice claims for their identities to be recognised and accommodated in the public space'. The present study is, effectively, a contribution to such a discourse. The goal is to allow the *different* voices of young people to play a part in the discussion of what schools fit for children might look like, physically and in terms of organization, in terms of learning and teaching, and in terms of social justice. These different voices need to be heard alongside those of adults. In particular there need to be mechanisms by which they can be heard by teachers, school principals and policy-makers.

Our study was an explicit consultation, and students were aware of our intention to share their perceptions of school in an anonymized form with their schools and teachers. Arnot and Reay (2004) refer to 'a cacophony of competing voices' in their study of young people's classroom experiences. Theirs was not an explicit consultation, aimed at directly informing teaching within the schools they examined. It differed in this respect from the work of Jean Rudduck (Rudduck et al., 1996; Rudduck and Flutter, 2004).

One of the challenges in analysing different perspectives within an explicit consultation is how to present these differences; in particular, how to handle opposing and contradictory viewpoints. For example, it may appear to the researcher that a particular viewpoint reflects a blind spot by the group of students concerned. Some students may come to completely opposite viewpoints about an aspect of schooling, such as whether or not wearing a school uniform promotes equality between students or directly hinders learning since teachers choose to focus on it instead of focusing on issues central to learning. At certain times, students may express opinions that reflect intolerance, or anti-democratic views. In a regular research account these issues can, of course, be discussed. But how should they be handled in a consultation? Equally importantly, how does a consultation allow for the perspectives of marginalized groups to be heard?

This study places emphasis on negotiation and on the development of a democratic dialogue between students and between students and the adults who work with them. While negotiation and democratic dialogue do not always provide neat solutions, they should ultimately generate increased understanding of alternative perspectives and a self-awareness that allows each of us to understand how our perspectives are situated in our particular life experiences and are effectively limited to a greater of lesser degree by those experiences.

Ultimately, democratic communities need to respond to the needs of minorities. Unless some kind of working accommodation is found, such groups will not be able to claim their human rights on the basis of equality with mainstream society. Democracy needs diversity. Without alternative perspectives there would be no need for democratic procedures and the democracy would stagnate. These are issues that school communities need to engage with and respond to.

Physical environment

There were many student comments about the design and state of repair of the buildings, the degree of comfort (relating to space and overcrowding, furniture, temperature control), classrooms (size, decor, brightness, furniture), and general cleanliness and hygiene. These were given as responses to the open-ended question in the survey, where students were invited to comment on factors that would support them in their learning or make school a more enjoyable experience. For many students, these features are stressed and discussed in detail and are said to have a significant impact on their capacity to learn.

Space

One of the biggest challenges facing students was lack of space. They spoke of crowded corridors and hallways, dining rooms and classrooms. One student wrote: 'School would be more enjoyable if there is less hassle when going into school buildings' and this kind of sentiment was common across all schools. Sometimes trouble broke out between students, because of this lack of room to manoeuvre.

They asked for bigger classrooms, so teachers could move around and help everyone more easily, and so that where necessary there could be two teachers to support everyone. Some students also believed that a shortage of classrooms sometimes determined class size, believing it was the number of classrooms, rather than the teacher–student ratio, which pushed class sizes up to 30. Students tended to agree that 20 was the optimum number for both sharing ideas and individual teacher support. At every school there were requests for smaller classes to enhance learning.

At one school students complain of a 'prison' environment. The school field appears to have been divided from the buildings by a fence and gates. Students write: 'Get rid of fence', 'move fences further away'. They argue that there should be no fences or gates, so that they can use the fields. One suggests that they need 'independence, not locked into small areas'.

At another school on an inner-city site, which has very small playing fields but large playgrounds, students request 'Grass to play football, so students wouldn't get hurt' and 'so it would be more fun'. Suggestions for improving the outdoor environment included a garden, picnic benches in the grassy areas, and more plants and flowers, although the individual asking for flowers added: 'they would probably get beheaded'.

Cleanliness and hygiene

Concerns about cleanliness (classrooms, hallways, dining rooms, toilets and changing rooms) feature in responses from students in all 13 schools in the survey. In five schools, 10 per cent or more of the student body consider that unhygienic and dirty conditions affect learning.

For example, problems relating both to the state of the toilets and access to them are raised by 12 per cent of the sample, receiving 226 mentions. They are a cause for concern among students in all schools across the city. Around three out of four complaints are expressed by girls, and although these concerns are expressed across ethnic groups, levels of concern appear highest among Indian students. Of greatest concern appear to be levels of hygiene, but other issues also come to the fore.

At Green Lane Community College (where OFSTED acknowledged student concerns and agreed with them that toilet facilities were appalling) students asked for basic refurbishment of toilets, pointing out they needed toilet rolls, improved hygiene, mirrors and 'doors where they should be', arguing that when facilities are good students respect the environment, whereas when they are inadequate, they take less care. In the student workshops conducted at Green Lane, students took photos of the toilets, writing captions such as this one by Farah and Sinita:

> The toilets are appalling and annoying because they are in a terrible state.

> No one likes to use them because they are so dirty. There is no decent toilet paper and the locks are broken.

Access to toilets

At another school nearly a quarter of all students raised concerns. In this school it appeared that the toilets remained locked before school and during lessons, being opened for mid-morning break and lunch only. Other requests across a variety of schools were for soap, 'proper toilet paper, not tracing paper', 'sanitary machines', 'being allowed to go to the toilet in lessons, as it is a human right' and ensuring that toilets do not 'always smell of smoke'. Students explained that 'some students are put off going to the toilet' and hinted that this might be a reason to stay away from school, particularly for girls, when menstruating. They requested locks and the need 'for privacy'.

In a minority of schools access to toilets was an issue of considerable concern. In addition to the school that kept toilets locked for a greater part of the school day, there were others where they were inaccessible during and between lessons, or where some but not all facilities were locked.

Students expressed frustration at the lack of respect shown to them, and at the embarrassment and indignities this caused.

At Long Meadow School a new building programme had resulted in new toilet facilities in one block. The students at this school made very few complaints, even though facilities remained unpleasant elsewhere on the campus. In the workshops students were quick to acknowledge what a difference this had made to morale, pointing out that all students, including those with disabilities, could now access the same high-quality facilities according to need, rather than be segregated, and captioning photos:

> Nice clean toilets only in G block.
>
> Mohammed

> Toilet facilities for people with difficulties (disabilities), absolutely tidy.
>
> Priya

Security

Toilets were an area where a number of students felt unsafe. Given that the students surveyed were among the oldest, this raises questions about the vulnerability of younger students to threats and bullying. Students in a number of schools request greater supervision of toilet areas, pointing out that teachers and other adult supervisors do not venture into them. One student suggests that the school should install 'cameras, so that anyone messing around can be punished' although other students challenge the use of CCTV in their schools, arguing that their privacy is compromised.

Other suggestions for improving the external physical environment of school include practical and inexpensive ideas, such as placing litter bins in recreation areas, in the dining hall and on the school field. Some students request 'benches with roof to stop rain', and more or better shelters.

Decor, repair and comfort

Within classrooms students highlight other concerns relating to both decor (quality of decoration, colours, brightness) and temperature control (heating, air conditioning, warmth, air flow). Concerns about the attractiveness and colours of classrooms were strong across all schools. It would appear that many schools were in need of internal decoration – 'it needs a lick of paint', but also that young people have strong preferences for bright colours:

- Tidy up classrooms so we feel like learning in them rather than scribbling on them or messing about.
- We need colourful bright rooms.
- It would be better if we had proper classrooms, not mobile classrooms.
- Good, clean classrooms help students work harder and they are more exciting and fun to be in.
- Classrooms need to be full of colour.
- There should be more flowers around school and interesting pictures and fact files on the walls.

Some students were able to identify positive examples of attractive learning environments, where teachers had taken an initiative to brighten up the school, such as the 'modernized' language department in one school.

Students at Green Lane Community College workshop told us they were ashamed to show visitors around the school, and pointed out that the library, where we met with them, was exceptional in having attractive displays and comfortable seating. They also felt that the school entrance and façade to the road (which was ugly) was embarrassing; it stopped them showing off their school to family members when they visited from other cities. While they clearly took pride in the school, and its achievements, they felt the poor fabric of the building was depressing and demotivating. They enjoyed those classrooms where teachers had displayed student work or made posters that gave hints on approaches to study. These efforts by teachers were hugely appreciated and did more than brighten up the tired decor, as these explanations attached to workshop photos testify:

> I think display work can be very important and fun, because it's showing off work you've done well, and making it look its best. Posters that help in class. It's good to have simple reminders of education around school to help with work.
>
> Farah

Another student at Green Lane suggested 'happy colours would help' and that putting 'more design into school would make it look respectable'. This viewpoint was echoed by a student at another school who proposed that students should be involved in the redesigning of classroom interiors.

From a student perspective, classrooms did not only need to look attractive they also needed to be much more comfortable and clean. This meant:

- getting rid of graffiti from exam tables;
- removing chewing gum from under tables;
- replacing old stools with chairs that provide back support;

- ensuring classrooms were big enough to accommodate the size of the class;
- providing adequate heating in winter and adequate air flow in summer.

The following comments are typical:

- We need a warmer school.
- Rooms need to be properly heated in winter.
- Air conditioning would help.
- School would be better if we had windows that open.
- What's needed is double-glazed windows (in old blocks). School would be much more enjoyable if we had a controlled working environment and better working conditions.

Flexible school day

Students at 12 of the 13 schools in the survey suggested changes needed to be made to the school day. By far the most common request was a later start, with students suggesting that they would not be so tired in the mornings, they would 'have more energy to learn', and it would allow both students and teachers to 'concentrate in the first few lessons', 'have time to get organized', and eat breakfast before arriving at school. They also argued the number of latecomers would be reduced.

Students commonly suggested a start time between 9–10 a.m. Sometimes students who requested later starts also requested an earlier finish or a shorter school day, but this was not always the case. A much smaller number of students requested an earlier start, with one citing the case of Germany, where he asserted that studies showed an early start and early finish was more effective for learning.

There were requests for Friday to be a half day, both from Muslim students who wished to attend prayers and from others who felt this would enable them to engage in more private study and cope with the volume of coursework/homework that they had to arrange. Some students even proposed a four-day week so as to allow greater time for assessed coursework. At one school, with a substantial Muslim population, there were requests for an extended lunch break on Fridays to allow students who wished to attend Friday prayers: 'It would allow time to pray Namaaz properly' and mean 'things don't have to be rushed'.

There were numerous requests across the schools for shorter lessons, with students claiming that very few people were able to concentrate for a full hour. The contrary view that lessons should be longer 'so students have more time to do quality work' was only raised by one student. Many students asked for a short (five-minute) break between lessons, particularly as many were not allowed to leave the classroom during lessons to use the toilets. It was also suggested a short break might 'refresh minds'. Others, and this trend was much stronger among girls, suggested shorter breaks so students could leave early and get on with coursework/homework at home.

It was clear that many students placed considerable emphasis on the social aspects of school and for this reason they proposed longer breaks and time to relax. A number asked for free periods so that they could access the library or computers. Another request was for longer library opening hours, and for school buses to leave a little later so that students could stay for an extra hour to do homework or join in extra curricular activities.

A few students proposed a flexible school day. Given the contradictory requests relating to school working hours, this topic was one that the research team raised in the online discussion. Students were asked to discuss the statement:

> The school day should be flexible, so that if a student wants to make a late start and work on into the evening they can do so.

The idea was generally warmly received by students, with broad agreement that it was a good idea to give pupils greater choice. Students did however identify a number of difficulties in implementing this idea:

> Flexibility sounds like a great idea, it would certainly stop all the complaints I hear from students regarding the length of the school day. There are, in my opinion too many problems with this though: satisfying both staff and students would be difficult; there are people who have autism or just anyone, who would rather stick to a set timetable; this would encourage anarchy as many students do not want to go to lessons anyway and if they didn't have to they wouldn't. This wouldn't stop skiving.
>
> Ian

> This is a very good idea for students who have problems in arriving to school on time due to family problems etc. Whereas other students would take it as an opportunity to deliberately come to school late and miss lessons.
>
> Shabana

> This is an excellent idea that would be very useful to have . . . The only problem would be lunch and break times but I would like to see this tested out.
>
> Daniel

I think this is a great idea. You can do work at a time that suits you, which means that our work would be of the best standard.

Chandni

In England the government is promoting and developing extended schools that might provide a range of services and activities, beyond the school day (DSCF, undated, *Extended Schools*). It is encouraging all schools to work with local partners to develop these services although it is not clear that students are recognized as potential partners. Nor is it evident that these students were aware of such proposals. The students' suggestions are in some ways more radical than official proposals, and it is clear that they have ideas that might be usefully incorporated into the decision-making processes.

School rules and discipline

A number of students raised problems with school rules they felt were petty or irrelevant. Others suggested that some rules were too easy to break, with rule-breakers entering a subsequent downward spiral of punishments. A few students suggested that rules would work more effectively if negotiated with students, and so we put this point to the students participating in the online discussion:

School rules and class rules need to be negotiated with students. If students help draw up the rules they are more likely to keep them. Schools where pupils are properly involved in decision-making are almost non-existent. How does your school measure up? What good ideas have you got?

This happens in some of my classes but rules are still not kept to.

Daniel

School rules are sometimes harsh. They may be there for the students to be able to learn more efficiently and more constructively. Although these rules are here to help stop bad students from disturbing the learning of others, some students that usually are well behaved and don't get into trouble sometimes get punished too harshly. For example, at my school, if you are late more than five minutes, three times a week, they automatically get a one hour detention. The teachers don't usually listen to the students and they just mark them late. Although this happens, this rule has been changed through negotiation. First, it used to be that you only had to be late once and get an hour's detention. Negotiation is the way of changing school rules for the better.

Jatin

This is a fantastic idea as most people will follow it as it is their choice and they have their say. Our school has just recently set up a new 'CONSEQUENCE' system, C1 and C2 are verbal warnings and C3 is an hour's detention and C4 is a day in isolation. We (student council) have been consulted and were asked about ours and the students viewpoints, and it is going to be evaluated.

Mohammed

This is a good idea because if the students get to choose the rules they are more likely to stick to them. In our school we discuss issues with the student council and then the headteacher. Everyone gets a say to what they think about rules and guidelines. It's a fair system!

Saab

Sometimes the wrong students get punished and no-one knows!

Rahul

Our school rules are made by the school and have nothing to do with students. Therefore problems are caused between the students and teachers. School rules should be made by students and teachers so the rules are fair.

Shabana

Our school's rules are very rarely enforced. There is a 'drop down' system which aims to expel the disruptive students from the classroom; this sort of system never works at our school. However, bigger rules that are broken are enforced and the best possible punishments (for the victim and offender) are given. These problems very rarely affect classroom activities and it is the ones that do that aren't dealt with. ... if the students breaking the rules are disrupting the class, there is a difference and this should be addressed.

Ian

School rules was one topic about which all the online contributors had plenty to say. Student councils were judged by a number of students to be a good mechanism by considering different viewpoints and evaluating how effectively the rules work in practice. Jatin's observation that 'teachers don't usually listen to the students' was one that was made again and again in questionnaire responses. It was applied particularly to questions of justice and to observations about discipline, but extended to all aspects of school life including classroom learning.

Students distinguish between breaches of rules that appear to harm no one (for example, chewing gum); those that hurt individuals; and those that disrupt learning. No one criticized rules or the implementation of rules that were designed to support purposeful learning, except where whole classes were punished for an individual misdemeanour, or where there was a perceived injustice or application of the rule in question.

There was a division of opinion on how purposeful learning for all could be realized. Some students, particularly girls, proposed that the school 'Separate the classes for people who want to learn and those who don't. In classes we get quite a disturbance by troubled students which distracts us (i.e. boys)' whereas others asked for more mixed ability teaching: 'Don't separate out less brainy people' and felt that problems would be eased if there was less pressure and 'by not having tests and coursework in different subjects at same time'.

Uniform

Students at all but two of the schools wore uniform. In these two schools there were lone voices proposing uniform on the grounds that it created a smart image, helped create a sense of belonging and reduced peer pressure. This perspective was also expressed in the online discussion where the topic was violence, bullying, racism and sexism. Priya wrote:

> We don't have uniforms in our school, but I think that having uniforms will stop a lot of bullying and violence. In my opinion, a lot of bullying is caused by clothes. For example, some people cannot afford to buy expensive clothes and others can. This can lead to bullying. By having uniforms, we will have equality and it will give an end to bullying, hopefully.

Her comments attracted support from another student in the same school:

> Yeh, I agree with Priya. Having uniform will give a sense of equality among students and will cut down bullying.
>
> Durgha

Within the survey for the majority of students who did not wear uniform, it was simply not an issue.

At all the other schools, some students complained about uniform, mostly on the grounds of comfort. At six of the schools, students argued that issues arising from uniform seriously hindered the primary business of the school; namely teaching and learning. It was said to cause unnecessary tension between students and teachers. Students advocated either relaxing uniform rules or abandoning uniform altogether since 'it makes us happier and stops the teachers complaining'; and it interferes with learning because enforcing it takes 'at least 15 minutes at the start of lessons'.

A number of students argued for more comfortable options without ties. Some students also objected because they suggested uniform hindered their self-expression and because they had little say in the design and choice of styles, colours and levels of formality that their school imposed. At two schools, in particular, it appeared to be a major source of tension and resentment. Students all appeared to enjoy non-uniform days, and requested more of these.

Meals

Across the city students spoke of difficulties relating to the lunch break and to school meals, including cramped dining facilities, spending the lunch break queuing, nowhere to relax (many requested a common room), and subsequent disorder and tensions between students. At some schools there were requests for canteen facilities to be available at morning break and before school so that students could buy breakfast if needed.

There were also concerns about the price of food, following a recent price rise, and requests for cheaper food. A number of those entitled to a free meal said that they could not get enough to eat from their allowance, largely because the price rise had not been matched by an increase in their allowance. One suggested that free schools meals should extend to £5 per head; another simply asked for a free meal and some students requested free milk or orange juice. Another wrote, 'If I am to learn effectively, I need cheaper food, so I can afford a decent meal'. A number of students were aware of the educational maintenance allowance (EMA) paid to students at age 16 plus, and thought the scheme should be extended to themselves.

Although there were some requests for junk food and fizzy drinks, which had recently been taken off the menu in schools across the city, the vast majority of specific requests were for more variety (and a changing daily menu), well-cooked food, and healthy options, including salads, fruit and low-fat meals. Some students even suggested items for the menu, such as curry, chow mein and noodles.

At particular schools there were complaints about the cleanliness of the trays and cutlery and requests for halal, Asian and vegetarian options. Other requests were for hot drinks and vending machines, and at one school cookery classes at lunchtime. A number of students pointed out that 'Students can only work properly with the right food and right amount'. A number of students requested more things to do at lunchtime.

Lockers

At some schools lockers were provided for all, but at seven schools, students requested them 'so we don't have to carry work around with us all day', 'so we have somewhere to keep PE kit' and so 'we don't break our backs'. Students pointed out that lockers would help them to be more organized and suggested they would improve their chances of bringing the right books to lessons. Students were aware of budgetary constraints, with one suggesting they could share facilities if cost was the issue. Budgetary restraints appear to have been made clear to students, probably by teachers, and one student observed: 'It would be fairer if all schools were funded the same and not played against each other'. This comment reflects an awareness among a minority of students of the ways in which schools are competing in a quasi-market to attract students and to access funds for specific projects.

Extra curricular activities, recreation and additional support

Students across the city requested opportunities both to extend their education and to engage in social and sports activities. A number asked for homework clubs and for additional learning support after school. There were requests from some schools to visit colleges and universities and to have better and tailored information about work and training opportunities.

Many students request better facilities for physical education with the suggestion from one student that her school is particularly badly provided for in this respect: 'Because it is a girls' school, there is nothing'. Other students at the same school requested a swimming pool, basketball and tennis courts. Another request, specifically from girls, is hairdryers in changing rooms. Students of both sexes request mirrors in changing rooms and showers that are divided into cubicles.

At Long Meadow School, where 90 per cent of students are of Indian heritage and where the school has a very stable population, the level of demand in the survey for extra-curricular activities, both during lunchtimes and after school, was exceptionally high. The school has a tradition of consulting students and promoting democratic engagement, and so it might be expected that the exercise would be taken very seriously. This was borne out in the detail of information relating to both classroom and beyond classroom experiences. Taking this into consideration, the level of demand for extra-curricular activities remains exceptional. The research team discussed this with student council members during the research workshop, and it was clear that school was seen, perhaps more so than in other schools, a centre of social activity and fun, as well as learning.

Interest in sports was very high indeed particularly, but by no means exclusively, among boys. Indeed, at Green Lane Community College, there was a plea from one girl 'to provide more sport for girls'. Students at Long

Meadow requested sports activities with the explicit purpose of bringing young people of different ages together, with requests for tournaments, a sports day, and other whole school events such as concerts 'so that all years can join in together'. Although the school appeared to have a strong sense of community, there were requests to strengthen this further. Equally important were non-sports clubs. After school and lunchtime activities were regarded by students as essential aspects of school; as one student put it, it helps 'to keep me interested'.

Students at Long Meadow also requested support with social skills, emotional support and efforts made to deal with specific problems, such as extra encouragement for the shy, and help with anger management. One student also asked 'to learn to make friends'. Another request was for 'more health checks'. It was argued that these kinds of support were needed 'for students to realize their full potential'. These themes were echoed in other schools across the city. At the only Catholic school in the survey, there was also a plea for sex education. Other additional curriculum requests included drugs awareness lessons.

Teachers and academic needs

Students also requested 'more experienced supply teachers' who had knowledge in the subjects they were studying. There were specific requests at Long Meadow for 'more black teachers' and 'more teachers from different ethnic groups and of different ages'. Students said a more representative teaching force would help them 'learn with/from teachers'.

General academic requests at Long Meadow included the chance to learn more languages, and more help or advice available in learning English. There were further requests for language learning from students at other schools, and these requests seem to come primarily from students who are themselves bilingual. It is not always clear whether they wish to study and take exams in a language they already know; but this seems likely in many cases, as when the request is expressed 'so it will help us with our GCSEs'.

Other requests included:

- more rooms to do homework at lunchtime (the library was already available and full at lunchtime on the days we visited);
- revision classes;
- more support for both those who found work difficult and those classified as 'gifted and talented';
- support for those who found academic work difficult.

What was particularly interesting is the way that a number of students extended writing about their own needs to looking at the needs of others.

Students at Long Meadow suggested that religious education and social issues are or should be 'a bigger part of education' and stressed the need for students to be able 'to understand their own cultures well as others'. Some students requested, as did students at other schools, that they be given more opportunities to orientate themselves to their future by 'more work experience and community service'.

At other schools it was argued that religious education should not be compulsory. Religious education remains a compulsory subject in England, although parents have the right of withdrawal. In an increasingly secular but multi-faith society, it has been justified both in terms of its contribution to moral education and to understanding perspectives of those from different belief systems (White, 2004). It is not clear whether students were aware of the parental right to withdraw their children.

As highlighted above, students across the city were aware of budgetary restrictions, with one student writing: 'I would be able to learn more effectively if the school had money to spend on the things it needs'. Others had viewpoints on the ways end-of-year surpluses had been invested to enhance student facilities and suggested that students should have been consulted in the processes of decision-making, so that 'future students could benefit' from wise choices.

Extending learning

Across the city a large number of students requested more school trips, both to make school more enjoyable and to support learning in the classroom. At Long Meadow, for example, there were requests for a skiing trip, visits to other countries, museums, and trips relating to 'specific subjects, such as science'. Reasoning behind the trips include 'to link we have learnt to real life experiences/happenings'; 'to help students learn better about the topics they are learning about'; and 'to encourage students to work harder'.

The research team noted how students generally saw school as a centre of their community/the local community and how some suggested school should be open to adults as well as children. We sought to follow this up in the online discussion, with the following prompt:

> Schools are too inward looking. They need to be open to adults as well as children. Young people need opportunities to study through visits, work placements and projects.

Students characteristically sought to explain what needed doing by drawing on their personal experience, while at the same time being sensitive to teacher perspectives:

Some teachers are worried about being sued if anything happens on school visits so there are less visits available to students. So far in secondary school I have only been on one trip and I'm in year 11.

Rahul

I think our school is very good on extended learning. There are many after school activities and I've been involved in two video production projects. One about learning to respect others, and [the] second learning about our heritage. This was provided through the youth workers who worked at our school last year.

Also if you are on the gifted and talented list there are loads of activities you can be involved in. Trips to universities and colleges are always good even if it's your local uni or Cambridge.

Durgha

Facilities and equipment

Students at different schools highlighted particular facilities and equipment, both academic and sporting, which they believed would make school a better place and enhance their learning and enjoyment. A number acknowledge that managing budgets demands a process of prioritization, and again request that they be involved in decision-making. So, for example, some students were critical of investment in electronic whiteboards or Astroturf, suggesting the money should be spent on books and equipment from which a greater number of students may benefit.

Although some requested opportunities to play computer games, most spoke of the need for access to the Internet in relation to school work and coursework requirements. More laptops were frequently requested and some students specifically requested the opportunity to rent laptops 'so people who haven't got [their own] computers can use them'. Repeatedly the point was made that the 'better the equipment, the more it motivates students to work' and this was applied to science laboratories, art rooms, and across the school. As one student put it: 'I would be able to learn more effectively, if I had the right equipment'.

Home access to textbooks and study guides was a common request: 'We should be allowed to take home study guides'; 'I would be a better student if I had textbooks to take home'. Some students also requested textbooks that were easier to understand and 'that explain everything'. Students across the city also commented on school libraries and asked that they be extended to represent a wider range of curriculum areas, suggesting that some subjects, such as maths and science, were inadequately supported.

Other requests were for more 'sports equipment for girls' and more up-to-date facilities in gyms and sports halls. There were also occasional special requests that all students should be able to access facilities that were only available to those who could pay, such as the request for 'free musical instrument lessons'.

One further request that was made across many schools was for 'usable drinking facilities', 'water fountains' and 'free water' available in communal areas or classrooms. At least two schools had school radio systems where music was played in communal areas and corridors at break; this was very popular and there were requests from students at other schools who wished this service to be extended to them to aid relaxation and reduce stress.

Individual support

In all schools it was apparent that a significant number of students accepted responsibility for their own learning and for creating an atmosphere that was conducive to living together in a community. So they were ready to point out that school would be a good space if they had 'a good attitude' and that what was needed was 'people being friendly to everyone'. Bullying was acknowledged as a difficulty in many schools, but in one in particular, there were a number of demands for help:

- Make people feel safe from bullies.
- I would be able to concentrate on learning if people who pick on me were expelled.
- I would enjoy school if people didn't pick on me.
- The school claims to have no bullies and [a] brilliant anti-bullying scheme but [has] quite a lot of bullies.

The issue of bullying is discussed further in Chapter 7.

There were requests from some schools for more teachers or assistants to be seen around the school, but at Long Meadow School, where a new school principal had recently employed a private security firm to supervise the corridors and hallways, students complained of insensitive treatment, hostility and racism from these individuals, both in the survey and in the student workshops.

A significant number of students made requests for individual support of various kinds and one noted that school would be better for her if 'my parents are welcome'. Better communication with parents was requested by other students at a range of schools, as in the comment: 'We would benefit from reports given every term to parents so they can see our progress or digression (sic)'.

Requests for support were in many forms; for example, 'It would help if school was more understanding of me'; 'I need more help in deciding choices GCSE'; 'We need help in deciding our careers', 'We should be able to express our feelings to people', and most poignantly, but frequently expressed: 'We need time to talk to teachers' and 'Let us talk to a teacher or a mentor at least once every two weeks'. In some schools the school nurse was appreciated as someone who would offer support and counselling. Clearly, one-to-one communication with an adult at school was seen by many young people as critical both enabling them to realize their potential and to enable security and well-being.

A number of students made references to the high levels of stress they and their friends experienced at school relating to academic pressures, claiming that teachers misjudged the pressure they applied in their efforts to ensure top grades for individuals and the school:

- I would do better if school wasn't made out to be as serious as it is.
- I would enjoy school much more if expectations were not so high and pressure was reduced.
- It would help not being reminded everyday about GCSEs.

These types of comment came much more frequently from girls and were made both in the girls' school and in co-educational institutions. Both boys and girls requested free periods when they could access the library and 'catchup' on work teachers assured them they were behind with. Work-related stress of this nature has been reported in earlier studies, notably among girls (Osler and Vincent, 2003).

Discussion

The Year 10 students in our study welcome the opportunity to comment on their schooling and are ready to give their opinions in the hope this might improve conditions for learning and enjoyment of school and help 'those in the future'. Students at some schools are clearly more regularly consulted than others and it is students at these schools who tend to provide detailed responses in the survey, more confident that their voices will be heard, listened to and acted upon. Others are not so sure as the following comment reveals: 'Please take into consideration what we have written and stop sending questionnaires because it is a waste of time'. This last comment was the only reservation about the survey that was expressed.

Although there were a couple of jokey references in the survey to 'teachers who need haircuts' and to 'those who come dressed in curtains', the comments are generally very respectful and students do not exploit the opportunity to complain about individual teachers or attack them unfairly. On the contrary, they show an understanding of teacher perspectives in their responses.

Although it is possible to identify some differences in perceptions of schooling needs by gender, what is striking about the responses is the common themes across the city and across ethnic groups. The most significant differences are between schools. So, for example, reported concerns about bullying, dietary needs and the organization of the school day vary between institutions.

It is also possible to detect particular concerns expressed by students from different socio-economic groups. Students raise concerns about the adequacy of the free school meal entitlement, access to laptops, revision guides and textbooks, pointing out they do not have these at home. There are also requests for specific support, such as free musical instrument lessons, affordable school trips that everyone can take up, one-to-one tutoring, and access to sports facilities. These are less problematic issues for middle-class students whose parents can supplement their schooling. A review of the overall sample reveals that the number of requests for further support are more common in schools that have a larger proportion of students from disadvantaged backgrounds (as measured by the uptake of claims for free school meals).

Although there have been considerable efforts by government to reduce child poverty in the UK, with targets set to reduce the numbers by one-quarter by 2004, most improvements were among those easiest to help; namely, children close to the poverty line. According to Magadi and Middleton (2005), 'children who were experiencing the most severe poverty had been left behind' or had not been reached by government's efforts. There remain therefore serious problems of *acute* child poverty.

In a more recent study for Save the Children on severe poverty, Magadi and Middleton (2007: 7) find that one in every ten children in the UK is living in severe poverty. They apply a measure of child poverty that combines a very low income (e.g. below 50 per cent of median) with severe material deprivation; that is to say, families deprived of particular 'child necessities' and 'adult necessities'. A total of 1.3 million children (10.2 per cent) have an income well below the government's poverty line and lack basic necessities that most people in the UK take for granted. It is these who are in acute poverty. The researchers report on the percentage of children in families who are deprived of specific child necessities that families would like but cannot afford. These include:

- 31.4 per cent who cannot take a week's holiday once a year;
- 10.6 per cent who would like but who cannot afford to go swimming once a month;

- 8.2 who cannot have friends round for tea or snacks once a fortnight;
- 5.1 per cent who cannot participate in school trips.

When we examine students' perceptions of schooling and what they believe they require to succeed at school in the context of these recorded national levels of child poverty, it is clear that the students' identified requirements for successful schooling are not in any way whimsical: without access to these facilities many of the young people will experience high levels of social exclusion and are unlikely to be able to benefit fully from the academic benefits of schooling. The evidence students provide suggests that for many young people the wider conditions of schooling may have a significant impact on their readiness to learn.

Across the city students are concerned about the physical conditions in which they are required to work and point out that even their teachers, based in the same institutions, do not have to endure basic problems over adequate food, lack of recreational space, or access to drinking water. Teachers have common rooms with access to water, food preparation and toilets. They also have greater autonomy, and are free to make a range of decisions about their working day. Lack of access to basic entitlements leaves students feeling they are disrespected by the school authorities, and that the school is not listening to them. Ultimately, this may damage relationships between students and teachers, and negatively affect the learning of individuals and groups.

Perhaps the greatest concern these young people have is that their teachers are unaware of many of their problems and that teachers are also making decisions about issues the students themselves care about passionately. Not to be consulted about problems when you have insights that you believe are not shared by those making the decisions is, of course, deeply frustrating and adds to the stress of school life, impacting on relationships between students and between teachers and students. The concerns that these students express about their working conditions and the ways they believe these are affecting learning need to be taken seriously.

The students effectively link (inadequate) *provision* of services with their own non-*participation* in decision-making processes. Lack of consultation with students, and insufficient engagement with their perspectives not only causes frustration and resentments, but effectively contributes to a context where many students feel they are materially disadvantaged in ways that hinder their learning.

It is clear that many students in this study are subject to unsatisfactory physical conditions and poor hygiene at school that would be considered totally unacceptable for adult workers in their workplaces. Adult workers have unions who are prepared to mobilize on their behalf; children lack these. Restricted access to toilets, for example, leads to indignities and humiliation that young people themselves believe drive some of their peers to stay away from school. The fact that these conditions persist is a testament to the low status of children and young people in society, and cannot be unconnected with children's lack of political power, or influence through the ballot box.

These conditions, coupled with inadequate facilities, such as shortage of textbooks and limited access to the Internet, are a particular burden for children from lower socio-economic groups who are required to complete demanding coursework assignments for examinations. Those in acute poverty stress the need for all young people to have access to nutritious food and additional educational and recreational experiences, making clear the negative impact of their poverty on their learning.

This consultation highlights issues that few texts on teaching and learning address. This in itself is a testament to the claim that young people should be involved in decision-making relating to their own education and that their voices should impact on educational policy-making at all levels.

6   Students and learning

This chapter focuses directly on the classroom and on students' expectations of teachers and the curriculum. In the survey of students in 13 schools across a multicultural city in the English Midlands, students were invited to say how they could become more effective, successful learners and how school could be made more enjoyable for them. It is apparent in many students' responses that the two issues of learning and enjoyment were inextricably linked:

> To help me be a better student I would have to enjoy school, to help me really learn and excel in academic studies.
>
> Male Indian 327, School D

Other themes that run though the accounts are students' concerns about the future and that their learning is relevant to their plans and aspirations; a recognition of their own personal responsibility for learning; a desire to be more active at school and to have supplementary learning activities, like school trips, which are available to all, rather than to the highest achievers; the pressure students feel as they prepare for examinations and complete assessed coursework; a strong desire to be listened to and respected by their teachers; and concerns from some that their identities be recognized and respected by the adults at school.

They repeatedly ask teachers to be more innovative and engaging in their teaching styles. Many are aware of something of the wider political context of learning and the pressures on schools and teachers to achieve good results, and succeed in league tables.

Pedagogy

A strand of thinking that stresses the link between learning and fun runs strongly through the suggestions that students make for improving lessons. They ask for new and imaginative teaching:

> I'd like it if there were ... different and new ways to make learning in all subjects more fun that include students more.
>
> Female Indian 072, Long Meadow School

Have more equipment to make the learning more fun and interesting.

Female Pakistani, School B

Students also challenge teachers to be better listeners and to be readier to offer praise and encouragement rather than find fault:

I'd learn much better if the teachers picked up and praised us for all the good things we do that go unnoticed and not pick up on the tiny things we do wrong.

Female White British 014, School C

School would be greatly improved if we had more encouraging and understanding teachers who are prepared to listen to me . . . teachers assume because they find a task easy, you will too, despite their years of experience.

Female White British 018, School I

I'd be better motivated if academic successes were treated with as much respect as sporting achievements.

Male White Asian 148, Long Meadow School

Although traditionally schools have treated academic achievements as more important than sporting and artistic endeavours, this has not been the case for black students, who have often been stereotyped as good at sports, but as low academic achievers. The concern by this mixed heritage student at Long Meadow that his school fails to recognize academic achievements may reflect a degree of stereotyping by teachers and/or a peer culture among some groups of young men where it is not cool to achieve academically. At Long Meadow 94 per cent of students are from black and minority communities.

According to students, more active methods are critical to improved learning. These need to be matched by greater cooperation between teachers and students and by team teaching in spacious classrooms, where everyone benefits from individual teacher support:

It would help if teachers and students can work better together rather than just the teachers dictating to the students.

Male White British 228, School D

Provide classes that are bigger and spacious so they can have more working teachers in there . . . this is so all students are heard.

Female White and Asian 164, School E

I think I could be a better student if lessons were more 'hands on' as I am a kinaesthetic learner.

Female Other Asian 224, School F

> Instead of the teacher just talking and getting students to write things down, make the lessons more practice (sic) like acting out what we read, doing more work on the computers, watching videos, having reading and discussion sessions would make a much better connection.
>
> Female Other Asian 101, School H

> We should do more practicals, more trips etc., as by doing physical things I find it so much easier to remember the things I am learning.
>
> Female White British 222, School D

Students were aware of book shortages, but felt that teachers needed to prioritize the purchase of textbooks, which allowed them to study independently. Independent learning and research were valued by many students, who believed it was more effective than 'just teachers telling us':

> I think if the teachers spent more money on books and equipment rather than buying loads of white boards this would be worthwhile.
>
> Female Indian, School C

> It would make a huge difference if we were allowed to take books we use in lessons home to help us if we don't understand or forget. Also it would be a useful thing because I can sit at home and read to keep it in my head.
>
> Male Indian 204, School E

> I would learn more if we could find out our own things and do our own research.
>
> Male White British 171, School K

Curriculum

Students have rather less to say about the detailed content of the curriculum (other than about religious education, as discussed in Chapter 7) than they do about pedagogy, but they stress how it should be relevant to their lives outside school and to their future studies or employment. This theme is most strongly expressed by white boys in the study:

> It would be better if they would relate the things we learn in school to the real world instead of learning things, things that we never use again, or maybe even forget.
>
> Male White British 255, School D

We learn things we won't use. They're trying to get us into university, but a uni degree is worthless in the working world.

Male White British 018, School H

The issue of choice was also very important to students. This included curriculum choices related to future careers, options within subjects, and the focus of coursework for assessment:

We should have a choice in what we want to learn, especially in science.

Female White British, School C

If only . . . I had a chance to choose . . . I only wanted to do business studies but the school made me do Spanish. I am really bad at Spanish and this gets mixed up with other subjects like French. Now I am not sure if I'll pass either of my languages. This lessens my enthusiasm towards school and depresses me.

Male Bangladeshi 019, School F

The issue of choice was closely tied to a pervading theme throughout the whole consultation with students: they wanted teachers simply to *listen to students' perspectives* relating to the curriculum, as in other areas of school life:

We would be able to learn much better if the teachers listen to us on what we've got to say regarding the content we are taught in lessons and the coursework that we do.

Female Indian 2587, School G

Not only do students feel that they should have a say in the content of the curriculum but they feel that teachers should take steps to build upon what they already know:

School would be much better for me if teachers found out what we knew before teaching us.

Male White British 171, School K

Students were particularly sensitive to the pressure they believed their teachers were placing on them to succeed and interpreted this as a direct outcome of the pressure that teachers themselves felt for their school to improve in local and national league tables. A number suggested that this pressure was counterproductive and hindering learning:

We would have better lessons and learn a great deal more if there was less pressure for schools to be successful in league tables. I don't believe that examinations are proper evaluations of pupils' intelligence and make young people feel stressed.

Female White British 128, School H

Teacher characteristics and behaviour

The words that occur most frequently in relation to teacher attitudes and behaviour are respect and equality. Students expect reciprocity in teacher–student relationships and while they acknowledge the need to show teachers respect, they also expect respect in return. A number raise the issue of teacher abuse of power and express concern that when, in their judgement, a particular teacher abuses their power and authority, there is no means of redress. Others, particularly girls, feel that there is a tendency among some teachers to undermine the confidence and self-worth of certain students:

> School would be a much happier place if ... the teachers would not use their authority to undermine students.
>
> Female Pakistani, School B

> It would be a much more comfortable experience if students got a chance to voice their opinions with confidence [and] that teachers will not contradict them.
>
> Female White British 301, Long Meadow School

> I would feel better at school if teachers treated me the way they like to be treated.
>
> Female White British 002, School C

> School needs to change so that teachers give students the same respect as I give them.
>
> Female Other Asian, Green Lane Community College

Boys from a range of different ethnic backgrounds tend to express concern about the confrontations that can arise because teachers will not listen to their points of view. This feeling of injustice was also expressed by girls but much less frequently:

> I think by being respected for who I am and what I am will make me a better student.
>
> Male Other Black African 087, School D

> It would really help if teachers actually listened to my opinion.
>
> Male Traveller 031, School F

> My opinion should be heard out and ask the questions without getting shouted at.
>
> Male Indian 258, School G

> If you complain about the teachers no action is actually taken. If a teacher complains about you, you always get a report, warning

and a very big investigation. I have always wondered what has happened to equal rights?

> Male African Asian 056, School F

If the teachers listened to your point of view before jumping to conclusions or giving a punishment.

> Female Indian 072, School E

It is notable that all the above concerns are made by black, Asian and Traveller students and not by their white counterparts. It is possible that this reaction is a reflection of the different and sometimes harsher experiences of discipline and control to which research has shown such students to be subject (Blair, 2001) or to the related problem of teacher stereotyping.

Issues of fairness and non-discrimination are raised in a number of forms. Some students feel that once they have a bad reputation there is little they can do to redeem themselves with a particular teacher. Others feel that teachers favour clever students and those who conform. It would appear that certain aspects of schooling, such as trips and outings, are given as rewards for good behaviour in some schools in the city.

> School would be improved if teachers taught students equally not favour clever pupils.
>
> Female Indian 031, School A

> Give all students equal opportunities meaning more clever people won't get more opportunities.
>
> Female African Asian 007, School G

> I would be happier if teachers didn't discriminate against me, maybe because of a previous incident.
>
> Female White British 025, School C

> If the teachers didn't prejudge me or anyone else I would feel much happier at school.
>
> Female White and Asian 011, School C

> My wish is being able to be different without being moaned at by the teachers who want you to be a 'perfect' student.
>
> Male White British 204, School D

> Teachers do not judge you as a group BUT as an individual.
>
> Female African Asian 161, Long Meadow School

This last comment appears to be a response to what the student perceives to be teacher stereotyping. The young woman in question wants her teachers to acknowledge her individuality, rather than see her merely as one of a mass of young Asian women at Long Meadow.

Students want the same standards of justice and fairness to apply to themselves as to teachers:

> If we were punished as single people not as whole groups so that it avoids punishing innocent students, that would be much fairer.
> Female White and Asian 012, School C

> We should have equal rights (teachers and students).
> Female African Asian 163, School E

Student behaviour

A large number of students listed the individual behaviours that might enable them to be more effective learners, such as improve attendance, work harder, finish tasks set and complete homework on time. But a number also expressed concern about the behaviour of students who they felt prevented them from learning, disrupted classes, and took up too much teacher time.

> I would be able to learn if certain other people improved their behaviour as there are lots of disruptive people in my school who do not respect others and are rude to the teachers.
> Female White European 022, School A

> It would be a lot better if less time was spent on disruptive students but more attention paid to those who want to learn.
> Female White British School I

> If people don't mess around then everyone could get attention because all the people who mess around get the attention for help.
> Female Indian 040, Long Meadow School

Some students argued for a change in attitude from within the student body and seemed to suggest that peer pressure might make a difference to behaviour, while others felt the responsibility lay with teachers to change their approach, be more firm, or remove disruptive students:

> What needs to happen is for all of the students to share the same positive attitude towards learning and work as hard as they can.
> Male Indian 185, School D

> It would help if good students were rewarded for effort, not bad students being rewarded for good behaviour.
> Female White British 232, School F

If discipline meant discipline and punishments were carried out without failure, school would work better.

Male White British, School K

The people who mess about [should be] taken away so that I could get on better with my work ... it is not fair on me and the other pupils who want to learn and get on in life.

Male White and Asian 152, School K

Personal support

A few students used the survey to plead for improved personal and emotional support. They suggested that counselling and support should be available to help them cope with emotional difficulties and family problems. These students, all girls, were concerned that the school engaged the support of educational welfare officers or contacted parents directly without finding time first to talk to the student about problems such as attendance. They believed these kinds of intervention, without first engaging the student in discussions, were unhelpful.

I would like school to become more helpful and help us through our bad situation in our lives and sit and talk to us. Because school attendance is the main reason [why contact is made with parents] but teachers don't know whether the children are going through a bad time [and] emotional stress.... Teachers should talk to students who they are worried about and find out the main reason for missing school. Teachers shouldn't send letters home or tell the education welfare to send letters home without talking to the student who they are worried about.

Female African Asian 171, Long Meadow School

To make me a better student I think that we should get to talk to a teacher or a mentor, who gives us targets and tells us our achievements once every two weeks so that we know how we are doing.

Female Indian 216, School G

Other requests for support came in the form of career information and planning:

I would be able to be a more effective student if I knew all the options available after school in more detail, so I can do more work that prepares for the future.

Female Pakistani 222, School G

Spending priorities

In reporting on classroom learning and teaching, students did not simply look at the curriculum or the behaviour of students or teachers. They also gave some thought to spending priorities and to the ways in which the school appeared to prioritize particular facilities. At school F, which had recently seen considerable investment in new, better equipped classrooms with improved technology, two students seemed to believe that spending was wrongly directed, since there were more basic needs to be met:

> This school would be a lot better if it stopped focusing on all its equipment and facilities and focused on bringing in some decent teachers instead of more computers.
>
> Male Traveller 050

> School would be a better place if money was invested in better ways. [School F] tends to spend its little money on building and on unnecessary extensions i.e. extra classrooms when there are plenty already. That money could be used on refurbishing class-rooms, new tables, chairs – comfortable even, not tacky plastic ones, new carpets etc.
>
> Male White British 023

Discussion

There is a high degree of consensus among the young people in this study about what constitutes the ideal conditions for learning. Learning needs to be *purposeful*; that is, it needs to relate to their lives beyond school and to their future plans, as well as enabling them to address the requirements of examinations and assessed coursework. Learning also needs to be *active* by which the young people mean that they wish to engage with each other and with the material, rather than be instructed by teachers. A good teacher is one who is innovative and who is prepared to introduce a range of methods into the classroom. They generally largely expect learning to be a *social* and *cooperative* activity. They seek opportunities to learn beyond the walls of the school and educational trips are highly significant in their school lives. In these respects the findings are consistent with the findings of earlier studies (Rudduck and McIntyre, 2007).

What is particularly interesting are the barriers to learning that the young people identify. As well as some more predictable barriers relating to the presence of unwilling and disruptive students, a recognition that they themselves are responsible for their own learning, and the observation by some that they do not always commit themselves wholeheartedly to study, there are additional barriers related to the ethos of schools and the pressures for schools to perform well in local and national league tables. Ironically, students perceive these pressures as stress and feel that they do not necessarily have the supportive encouragement from teachers to succeed.

A second barrier relates to perceived injustices by teachers. If the conditions of school seem unfair as a result of teacher stereotyping, prejudice, or lack of respect for young people, then students feel undermined. They strive to be autonomous individuals and, to a greater or lesser extent, autonomous learners, engaging in research individually or in groups.

Finally, they are critical of school norms that do not allow them to engage with their teachers to determine the content of lessons and to discuss their learning needs. For these young people, very few of whom have had the opportunity to be consulted about their school lives or to participate meaningfully in school decision-making, a sense of powerlessness and lack of agency threatens the good efforts of individual teachers.

At Green Lane Community College and at Long Meadow School, students took photos to illustrate good teacher–student relationships. They showed teacher–student interaction in one-to-one situations, playing chess or deep in conversation. Some spoke of the family atmosphere of school, where their brothers, sisters and cousins were also part of the school community. Their ideal teacher was someone you could confide in, seek advice from, someone who was like an older sibling or cousin with whom you would feel at ease in talking. In referring to equality in teacher–student relationships, they are not asking teachers to give up their authority, but to use it wisely and to show respect to young people. Consulting them about their own learning and their own needs was a basic element in demonstrating respect.

7 Students and social justice

Children and young people do not simply have the right to education. The UN Convention on the Rights of the Child (CRC) in its Article 29 also specifies that children have the right to an education in human rights, which prepares them for democratic participation, and enables them for tolerant coexistence with people with different experiences, cultures, ethnic and religious backgrounds from their own. It speaks of the nation states obligation to promote education for peaceful coexistence with others in their communities, the nation and the wider world:

> States Parties agree that the education of the child shall be directed to ... The development of respect for human rights and fundamental freedoms ... [and] preparation of the child for responsible life in a free society, in the spirit of understanding, peace, tolerance, equality of sexes, and friendship among all peoples, ethnic, national and religious groups and persons of indigenous origin.

This implies some level of engagement with young people from backgrounds different from their own and a degree of educational integration between children from different backgrounds. This type of education, where young people are supported in learning to live together with difference at all levels from the local to the global, is what has been termed 'education for cosmopolitan citizenship' (Osler and Starkey, 2003, 2005).

Additionally, Article 29 continues, each child also has the right to an education that promotes:

> respect for ... his or her own cultural identity, language and values, for the national values of the country in which the child is living, the country from which he or she may originate, and for civilizations different from his or her own.

In other words, not only do children have a right to be educated for tolerance and for diversity, but they also have a right to an education that supports their own cultural heritage and that of their families' countries of origin, as well as the culture and values of the countries in which they are living.

This chapter considers potential tensions that may exist in practice between education for democracy and diversity (living and studying together) and those organizational arrangements that emphasize the child's own cultural heritage through the development of alternative systems of schooling. In particular, it will consider school systems and arrangements where children from particular cultural or religious communities are educated (to a greater or lesser degree) separately, and whether it is possible within such systems to genuinely create education for living together. Chapter 2 noted how the Committee on the Rights of the Child, in its 2008 report on the implementation of the CRC in the UK, expressed concern that the 'problem of segregation is still present in Northern Ireland' (Committee on the Rights of the Child, 2008: 15). The ways in which education authorities organize school systems is likely to be as important in guaranteeing children's educational rights as the classroom practices of their teachers.

This chapter reports on ways in which young people perceive their schooling to support preparation for living together with others in a spirit of peace, tolerance and equality. It also explores the degree to which they feel their education encourages respect for their own cultures, languages and those of others in their city and beyond.

One of the biggest obstacles to peaceful coexistence that students raise is bullying. The chapter will present findings relating to the impact of bullying on their lives.

Before analysing the young people's viewpoints and perspectives on education and social justice, the chapter briefly considers two issues that have a direct bearing on education for democracy and diversity, namely, the issue of faith schooling and multiculturalism.

Separate but equal?

At the time of the study, the city had just one Catholic secondary school, although around one-third of primary schools were church schools. All other publicly funded secondary schools in the city at that time were non-faith-based. From 2007, an established Islamic school moved from the private sector to receive public funding, and a new Christian academy was established, run by the Church of England. The balance of faith schools to non-faith has therefore changed substantially since the consultation with young people.

In the primary sector, church schools in the city are seen by parents as providing the highest standards and are consequently the most popular. Nevertheless, faith schools do not recruit proportionality across all socio-economic groups: they have fewer children entitled to free school meals and they also have fewer children with special educational needs than their non-faith counterparts. In this respect they mirror the picture elsewhere; faith schools in England tend to accept proportionally more middle-class children and their selection procedures have tended to disadvantage the poorest (West and Allen, 2008).

It is children of mixed heritage who are most often the reported victims of racial abuse within the city. City officials report that faith schools are often seen as a haven from racism and racist abuse. The city's primary schools are near the bottom of the national league tables in terms of students' academic attainment. As in a number of other local authorities, African–Caribbean children are among those for whom the city's schools can be said to be underachieving; this is true at secondary level as well as in the primary sector. African-Caribbean students leave school with lower average grades than their white peers.

Although the expansion of faith schools has been popular with many parents, and has been justified by the British government in terms of their academic success, the arguments for an expansion in their numbers may not be in keeping with efforts to promote children's rights, particularly children's participation rights. Research conducted by the Runnymede Trust (Osler, 2007; Berkeley, 2008), which set out to explore the contribution of faith schools to community cohesion and their impact, if any, on ethnic segregation, concluded that while faith schools cater well for parental choice and the rights of parents to educate their children in keeping with their own religious and moral convictions, there was little evidence that they were addressing children's voice or children's rights. It noted that faith schools appeared to give little attention to other aspects of young people's identities beyond faith identities and stressed how these schools need to engage more directly with children's perspectives on their schooling.

Grover (2007) argues that education for tolerance, in keeping with the provisions of Article 29 of the CRC, cannot be fostered where there is complete educational segregation. She concludes that it needs to 'be acknowledged that educating for peace will require states to mandate some level of educational integration of schoolchildren from diverse ethnic, religious, cultural and language groups' (Grover, 2007: 60). She calls on advocates of children's rights to recognize that the child's right to education is, legislatively and judicially, treated as a parental liberty right (to have the child educated according to parental wishes within the general minimum standards set out by the state). This tends to work against children's rights.

Grover also suggests that 'the notion of minority education is frequently erroneously translated into *completely segregated school systems'* (Grover, 2007: 61, my emphasis), which effectively offers no opportunities to integrate children from different cultural or religious groups. Here, examples might include post-conflict Northern Ireland, where the majority of children still attend either Catholic or Protestant schools, according to their families' religious tradition, or the ethnic and religious divide in schooling in countries of the former Yugoslavia, where separate schooling is justified in terms of continued parental mistrust following a period of war and so-called 'ethnic cleansing'. To agree to send your child to an integrated school in such contexts requires a strong commitment to peace that outweighs understandable fears about the individual child's well-being and the commitment of one's former enemies to the same goals. Integrated schools need to demonstrate a genuine commitment to inclusion.

So, for example, it might be argued that the education authorities in the Republic of Cyprus, where the curriculum and textbooks mirror those of Greece, should demonstrate their commitment to integration and the minority of Turkish Cypriot students by developing a specifically Cypriot curriculum and by requiring students to study Turkish as well as Greek, acknowledging the fact that both are official languages of the Republic of Cyprus, with Turkish becoming (and remaining) an official language of the Republic following the Treaty of Zurich in 1959.

Finally, Grover argues that the 'minority and non-minority child's legal right to free association (each with the other) in the education context is frequently disregarded both by the legislature and the courts' in nation states across the globe. She explains this in terms of the judicial and legal bias that exists in most nation-states in favour of parental rights, rather than those of children.

Parents' rights or children's rights?

Grover illustrates her points with reference to a number of seminal cases illustrating judicial perspectives on educational integration relating to religious and linguistic minorities and to children with special needs. In the cases she cites, she illustrates how the right to an education that prepares young people for living together is often trumped by parental liberty rights. So, in the case of *Wisconsin* v. Yoder *et al.* [1972] 406 U.S.205, the American Supreme Court ruled that Amish children could be removed from public schooling after completing only grade 8, denying them a right to educational integration with non-Amish children. In its ruling the Court stressed 'the *traditional interest of parents* with respect to the religious upbringing of their children' (quoted in Grover, 2007: 66, my emphasis). The court justified its decision in terms of the religious interests of the parents without reference to the human rights of the children in question. Grover points out that it would have been possible to provide some level of integration for Amish children in the mainstream schools while at the same time providing traditional Amish vocational and religious

education within the Amish community. The Court gave no consideration to the child's right both to educational integration and freedom of
religion or to freedom of association and linked rights such as freedom of
expression.

In another case affecting a minority group child's right to education in
an integrated setting, while maintaining his right to practise his religion
(*Multani* v. *Commission Scolaire Marguerite-Bourgeoys*), an orthodox Sikh
boy, who wished to follow the requirement of his religion to wear a kirpan
(small ceremonial knife) at all times, was barred by his local Canadian
school board from doing so. This resulted in the child being unable to
go to school. This effectively was segregation on account of the board's
denial of the child's right to practise his religion. This was despite the child
agreeing to wear the kirpan sheathed and under his outer clothing. The
Canadian Supreme Court ruled that these conditions would have ensured
the safety of fellow students, observing that there had been no instances
of a child using the kirpan as a weapon and pointing out that in all schools
there are, in any case, other instruments, such as baseball bats, which can
be potentially used as weapons. Importantly, the Canadian Supreme Court
also stressed the importance of education for *tolerance:*

> Religious tolerance is a very important value of Canadian society.
> If some students consider it unfair that G may wear his kirpan to
> school while they are not allowed to have knives in their posses-
> sion, it is incumbent on the school to discharge their obligation
> to instil in their students this value [tolerance] that is the very
> foundation of democracy
> (*Multani v. Commission Scolaire Marguerite-Bourgeoys* [2006],
> quoted in Grover, 2007: 66).

Despite the ways in which education policy is framed so as to guarantee parental liberty rights in their children's education, the courts may
rule in favour of children's rights. The case of *Plyler* v. *Doe* in the USA
affirms children's independent right to educational integration. In 1982
the Supreme Court ruled in favour of integration into the Texas school
system of children who were illegal aliens from Mexico. The Court made
the decision in the context of universal human rights; namely, the child's
right to education. This decision was made not withstanding the Court's
rejection of any parental liberty right to educate the child in a particular jurisdiction where the parent has no lawful status. In this case *Plyler
(Superintendent, Tyler Independent School District)* v. *Doe Supreme Court of
the United States [1982] 457 U.S. 202,* the American Supreme Court's decision was based exclusively on children's rights, and not undermined by
parental status or parental liberty rights. Grover (2007: 69) observes that in
this case 'implementing educational integration of lawful and unlawful

residents' was an indicator of the value the court placed on the role of education in promoting democracy and, therefore, tolerance.

In England there is a long tradition of religious involvement in publicly funded schooling. Faith schools constitute one-third of public sector schools. The vast majority of these schools are supported by the Christian churches, predominantly Church of England, but with substantial numbers of Catholic and much smaller numbers of Jewish schools. From 1998 these have been joined by Muslim schools, and, more recently, Sikh and Hindu schools.

The decision at the beginning of the twenty-first century to expand publicly funded faith schools in England might be seen as a step towards equality, guaranteeing the rights of parents from religious traditions other than Christianity to choose faith-based education for their children. Alternatively, since the numbers of Christian schools have also grown since this time, it might be seen as a step towards religious separation, particularly as the demand for faith-based secondary school places exceeds the number of places, and many such schools have operated an admissions criteria in a fashion that has been less than transparent and which has served to further disadvantage children who are already marginalized as a result of poverty or having special educational needs (House of Commons Children, Schools and Families Committee, 2009).

So as to mitigate the effects of a school system that does not guarantee integration, and in keeping with broader government polices relating to cohesion, from 2007 all maintained schools in England have a legal duty, under the Education and Inspections Act 2006, to promote community cohesion. Guidance to schools on how they can meet their legal duty to promote community cohesion states:

> By community cohesion, we mean working towards a society in which there is a *common vision* and a common sense of belonging by all communities; a society in which the diversity of people's backgrounds and circumstances is appreciated and valued; a society in which similar *life opportunities* are available to all; and a society in which strong and positive relations exist and continue to be developed in the workplace, in schools and in the wider community (DCSF, 2007: 3, original emphasis).

Publicly funded schools that are effectively mono-faith or monocultural are expected to develop linking arrangements with other schools, cooperating in the area of sports or the arts, so as to develop a degree of integration among their students.

The case in the CRC is for the child's right to an education that promotes tolerance. Nevertheless, the CRC is a minimum standard for all children, and it is useful to consider the limitations of the concept of tolerance and thus the notion of education for tolerance. Tolerance by all parties may be an essential first step towards the development of a successful multicultural society, but it is unlikely to be a sufficient requirement for longer-term development. It needs to be balanced by guarantees of equality of rights (also ensured in the CRC) and the absence of discrimination not just at the level of interpersonal relationships but also within the structures of government at national, local and community levels, in the workplace and in key services such as education and health.

Multiculturalism in Britain

At the time of our qualitative data collection in schools, in spring 2005, political and media rhetoric in Britain was increasingly critical of multiculturalism. From 2001, following the 9/11 attacks on the USA, such views began to be expressed. They attracted greater attention after the July 2005 suicide bombings in London. These events and their aftermath shifted the focus of political and media discourse on race relations in Britain. They have given an international dimension to public debate about diversity and belonging. Their impact continues to be felt in education. A range of commentators, including senior government ministers, have chosen to focus on the role of schools in creating a united and cohesive society and to suggest how the curriculum, notably the teaching of history and citizenship, might be directed to strengthen Britishness and British values (Osler, 2009b).

The emphasis, particularly in the case of adult migrants and aspirant citizens, but also young people, is on integration into the nation, but policies to ensure inclusion and integration (e.g. citizenship test requirements that require aspirant citizens to learn about mainstream British culture and achieve basic standards in English or Welsh) are not necessarily balanced by efforts to ensure respect for diversity, so that minority cultures, languages and traditions are respected and encouraged to flourish (Osler, 2009a).

Some government ministers have questioned Britain's multiculturalism and the then Commission for Racial Equality (CRE) Chair, later head of the Equalities and Human Rights Commission, Trevor Phillips, suggested that Britain needs to abandon a model of multiculturalism that is leading people to live separate lives. Phillips' (2005) warning, widely reported in the media, is that: 'we are sleepwalking our way to segregation. We are becoming strangers to each other, and we are leaving communities to be marooned outside the mainstream'.

Drawing on the experience of the USA and on the example of the poor and predominantly African-American victims of hurricane Katrina,

Phillips warned of the dangers of a segregated and unequal society in which the average black child attends a largely black school and the average white person returns home to a largely white suburb. In the USA, hurricane Katrina challenged the myth of integration based on black success stories, revealing that poor black people were both invisible to and forgotten by powerful decision-makers. Arguing that Britain has a different concept of integration from the USA, Phillips suggests that:

> for all of us who care about racial equality and integration, America is not our dream, but our nightmare. ...There I think the focus is purely on equal rights for different groups. Amongst America's hyphenated identities, the part of their identity that marks them out as different seems to have become as important, even more important, than the part that binds them together.
>
> (Phillips, 2005)

In Phillips' speech, as in speeches that were made by the then Prime Minister Blair (2006) and future Prime Minister Brown (2006) the following year, there is an emphasis on the shared values that bind the British together. Calling for a focus on these values (democracy, freedom of speech and equality) and on common traditions (a common language, good manners, care of children, ironic humour targeting politicians, priests and do-gooders), Phillips (2005) argues that diverse lifestyles compatible with these common values are fully accepted in contemporary Britain: 'No-one tells us how to speak, how to dress, what we should eat or how we should worship'. He argues against a model of multiculturalism that is relativist and which permits behaviour such as child cruelty and abuse in the name of cultural or religious freedom.

Phillips' critique of multiculturalism is that it disguises and neglects structural inequality and promotes segregation. One problem is that it has been taken up by media commentators and used to back a call for uniformity and assimilation. As a journalist, Phillips might have been expected to anticipate that his ideas would be taken out of context by those less concerned with equitable outcomes in order to attack initiatives promoting racial justice and to demand assimilation of minorities. In a context in which Islamophobia flourishes, this call for uniformity by sections of the media amounts to an attack on Muslims who are portrayed, as a number of writers have observed (Richardson 1997; Jawad and Benn, 2003), as a homogeneous group threatening 'our values' and 'our way of life'. In fact, structural inequalities and poverty go a long way towards explaining the segregation that exists in some towns and cities, for people do not necessarily choose to live in certain neighbourhoods but are constrained by a range of social and economic factors (Home Office, 2001).

A second difficulty lies in Phillips' claim that multiculturalism has failed. Britain has never had an explicit government policy of multiculturalism, such as that practised in Canada, for example. There is not an explicit, comprehensive policy to assess. For this reason, it is difficult to assert that the British approach to multiculturalism has failed. If multiculturalism has failed, it is logical to abandon it. If, however, Britain has experimented with imperfect forms of multiculturalism then these can, theoretically, be revised and adapted. But what has not been tried cannot be said to have failed.

At a local level multiculturalism has been adopted on a piecemeal basis. Education is one policy area where, until the establishment of a national school curriculum for England in the late 1980s, attempts were made in some local authorities to develop multicultural policies (Figueroa, 2004; Tomlinson, 2005). But these efforts were neither uniform, nor consistent across the country, and they were largely restricted to schooling. Multiculturalism cannot be blamed, for example, for a tendency towards segregation in parts of the university sector, a sector that Phillips rightly criticizes. Universities have been very slow to meet their obligations under the Race Relations [Amendment] Act 2000 (RRAA), and the sector as a whole has shown little interest in multiculturalism. There are huge disparities in student intake between universities: in 2004/5, 53 institutions had less than 5 per cent minority British undergraduates and 20 institutions had more than 40 per cent minority students. Half the prestigious Russell group universities had fewer than 30 black students of Caribbean heritage. London Metropolitan University had more black Caribbean students than the whole of the Russell group put together (CRE, 2007: 12).

A third difficulty in Phillips' critique lies in the appeal to common values, without identifying the basis of those values, and to common traditions such as a common language and the care of children. While Britain has a common language, it might equally be characterized as a nation-state comprising many bilingual and multilingual as well as monolingual communities. The evidence does not support a special British tradition of caring for children. The UK has been regularly criticized for its failure to protect and guarantee the rights and well-being of children and young people. A United Nations Children's Fund (UNICEF) report (2007) placed the UK bottom of an international league of developed countries for children's well-being, revealing considerable disparities between children in income and educational attainment. An appeal to common values needs to be explicit on the basis and source of those values, as in any society there are likely to be examples in which there are competing claims needing to be resolved. The shared values are those of the international community.

In Britain since 2001 there has been a significant shift in political discourse. On the one hand, there is an explicit new appeal to patriotism by Gordon Brown; on the other hand there are direct appeals by a number of political leaders, including Gordon Brown, to 'British values', which are directly referenced to British history and culture, but not generally acknowledged as the broad human rights principles to which the wider international community has committed itself, or as the shared values of modern democratic nation states. Equally significantly, within a nation state with a multicultural population, multiculturalism as a policy approach is presented as in crisis. This apparent crisis is closely linked to a broader public discourse in which Islam and Muslims are themselves problematized. While senior Labour figures have generally defined Britishness in an inclusive fashion, Muslims, and particularly Muslim women, are presented as a largely homogeneous community, the Other, which needs to adapt to the prevailing norms of a majority society.

The message for educators and the wider public, as reflected in the media, is that Britishness and the British story needs to be framed within narrow territorial boundaries. Outsiders need to learn British history in order to integrate into the community of the nation. British history is presented as a single, unproblematic narrative, rather than a complex process, reflecting the varied stories and perspectives of Britain as a 'community of communities' (CFMEB, 2000). Debates about national identity, as reflected in the popular press, have often been clouded by racist and Islamophobic sentiments (Richardson, 1997; Ameli et al., 2007).

There is no recognition of structural racism or its potential impact in undermining efforts to promote unity and integration in these key speeches. Policies that aim to strengthen a sense of belonging, either to the local community or to the nation but which fail to address deprivation, racism and inequality are likely to be met, at best, with scepticism. At worst they may further alienate those they seek to include. This is acknowledged by the government-appointed Commission on Integration and Cohesion (COIC, 2007: 21), which observes: 'Integration and cohesion policies cannot be a substitute for national policies to reduce deprivation and provide people with more opportunities: tackling inequality is an absolute precondition for integration and cohesion'.

Issues of diversity, democracy, patriotism and citizenship are given a new emphasis in response to the threat of global terrorism and to a perceived need to integrate Muslim citizens. Both Blair (2006) and Brown (2006) discuss the tension between diversity and integration, which they see as a particular challenge post-July 2005. The tension between policy initiatives that promote unity (cohesion) and those which support diversity is not confined to Britain for, as Blair acknowledges: 'we are not on our own in trying to find the right balance between integration and diversity. There is a global agonising on the subject' (Blair, 2006).

This is the broad context in which we can consider the implications of young people's perspectives on social justice for policy development, both at classroom and school level, and beyond. Their opinions on learning to live together and the degree to which their schooling addresses questions of children's rights and social justice follow.

Respect for religious beliefs

There were numerous concerns across the city relating to religious holidays and the opportunity to practise religion; in particular, the request from Muslim students that they be given time to pray at particular times during the school week. There were also requests for holidays to celebrate Eid and the Hindu festival of Navrati. These requests were usually expressed in terms of equity across all religious faiths represented in the school. Much of the data is drawn from our survey where students have selected an ethnic category from a predetermined list. The descriptors, such as 'Indian', 'White and Asian', 'Other Black African', are the ones used by the city authorities, which reflect and extend the categories used in the 2001 census.

> The school gives around two weeks holiday for Christmas, Easter (Christian festivals) then why don't the school give holidays for other religious festivals such as Eid etc.? Another point is that people (Hindus) who celebrate Navratri got a hour off in the morning as they were celebrating the night before till very late, when in fact Muslims who celebrated Ramadan, have to wake up at sunset (very early in the morning) they were expected to come on time. This should stop or it should be equal.
>
> Female Indian 032, School A

The request for a holiday at Eid was also made by students at schools K and G, with students suggesting that 'everyone gets two days off at this time'. As discussed in Chapter 5, Muslim students at some schools were given time for prayers on Fridays, but at other schools this was not the case, so that students at school F, for example, requested the chance to 'able to pray at certain times of week at certain times'. Since religious festivals are special occasions in many young people's calendars, a student at Green Meadow requested 'fun lessons when festivals take place', rather than a school holiday.

Such requests relate to freedom of religion and are about the degree to which students are able to practise their religion while at the same time being fully integrated into school life. So, for example, it would seem reasonable for the school to arrange occasional holidays to coincide with major religious festivals. Another consideration is the way that homework and coursework is set, to enable students to be able to fulfil their academic commitments, as well as their religious obligations. A number of students at the all girls' school C asked for the school day to be compressed, with fewer/shorter breaks, so that they could meet their religious obligations. These requests were expressed in terms of enabling their maximum academic potential and avoiding unnecessary stress:

> I would do better at school if I had more time at home to complete homework. I go to mosque from 5–8 pm. When I do my homework, I end up sleeping late and waking early to do mosque's work, resulting in stress.
>
> Female Indian 019, School C

Concerns about respect for students' religious practices were also expressed in terms of the need for greater tolerance within the community of the school by both students and teachers:

> School would be far more enjoyable for me if students would respect other students for who and what they are and believe.
>
> Female Pakistani 023, School B

For some students this was expressed in terms of a reorientation within the curriculum so that:

> RE and social issues are a bigger part of the education in order for students to understand their own culture as well as other peoples.
>
> Female, White and Black Caribbean 301, Long Meadow School

A student at school D suggested that this could be achieved in her view by 'events to learn about religious festivals organised by students'.

Not all students felt the need for further religious education to enable tolerance and understanding of diversity. A white student at Green Lane Community College argued: 'I think religious studies should be optional because some people don't believe in religion and I don't think they should have to learn about it'. This comment suggests the need for religious education that includes a study of secular traditions, and further discussion with students about the purposes of religious education, including the contribution it might make to greater tolerance and cooperation.

The need for tolerance is also illustrated by a request by a student from school A that St George's Day be given as a holiday. St George's Day has not traditionally been a public holiday and this request might be interpreted as a request for equity, since other students are demanding that specific festivals within the Islamic and Hindu traditions are observed. However, if this is the case, then the student would need to acknowledge, as some students point out, that key Christian festivals of Easter and Christmas are already marked by school holidays. It is also possible that the student has been influenced by mainstream politicians to promote 'Britishness'.

However, it may be the case that the student has been influenced by far right political propaganda in calling for a St George's Day holiday. The British National Party (BNP) has been active in the city and the wider Midlands region over a number of years. In June 2009 the BNP achieved the first parliamentary success of a far right party in Britain in the European elections with two Members of the European Parliament elected; one for the North West and the second for Yorkshire and Humberside. The BNP polled 8.6 per cent in both the East and West Midlands and although this was insufficient to secure a parliamentary seat in either region, it was a greater proportion of the vote than in the North West, where just 8 per cent was enough to return a parliamentary candidate (*The Guardian*, 2009). This suggests that teachers cannot afford to be complacent about the susceptibility of students to such political propaganda and that they have a duty to ensure that all students are educated for democracy and tolerance (Osler, 2009c, forthcoming).

In keeping with the judgment of the Supreme Court of Canada in the example given above, and in line with the right of all students to be educated for human rights and participation: 'it is incumbent on the school to discharge their obligation to instil in their students this value [tolerance] that is the very foundation of democracy'. This principle notwithstanding, the request from a student at school E that the school should develop 'work to suit every religion in the school, not just Asian people but other ethnic backgrounds' needs to be heeded, if all students are to feel that the curriculum is inclusive of themselves.

What is clear from the survey responses is that many students, particularly those in schools where the student population is drawn from many faith communities as well as from secular backgrounds, show considerable respect for others' beliefs and an understanding of others' religious needs. Among such students the right of others to exercise freedom of religion and be included in the school community is unquestioned. Some raise concerns that the school curriculum does not recognize secular lifestyles or acknowledge atheistic beliefs. Yet some students, particularly those in less diverse school settings, also show resentment and distrust of others' beliefs, and this is confirmed by the concerns of others that their identities and faiths are not respected. While it is a challenge to try to reconcile different demands, it is clear that increased dialogue between students of different faiths and between those who have a religious faith and those who do not will resolve some misunderstandings. Teachers too may have much to learn in such a dialogue.

In some nations, school is a religion-free zone. However, it is clear from international standards relating to freedom of religion that this acts as an exclusionary practice. It is important that all aspects of a student's identity are respected, including faith.

The challenge in faith schools is to recognize other aspects of young peoples' identities. As the Runnymede Trust report on faith schooling and community cohesion notes:

> Faith traditions often reflect and sustain gender inequalities in society that remain a source of contention within many religious communities. . . . faith schools should, like all schools, redouble their efforts towards valuing and appreciating diversity in terms of gender, ethnicity, disability, age and sexual orientation.
>
> (Berkeley, 2008: 39).

Efforts to promote tolerance and understanding of others need to be extended so as to address how people from different communities can live together. This implies a form of political education and critical evaluation skills based on human rights norms. As one respondent to the Runnymede Trust consultation acknowledged, knowing about others and even engaging with others will be insufficient:

> It is more important that young people are taught critical reasoning skills and are allowed to apply these to their own and other belief systems. Bland multi-cultural sharing without comparative analysis and critique only serves to create intellectual and social dissonance.
>
> (quoted in Berkeley, 2008: 38)

Teachers respecting students

One theme that runs through the students' responses is the need to be shown respect by teachers. Laura, a student at Green Lane Community College, acknowledged the need for reciprocity between teachers and students, but suggested this was also an issue for teacher education:

> Teachers should be taught about how younger people think and act.
> Teachers should be told and students that if you respect them you will earn respect back.

Students at Green Lane perceived a large gap between them and teachers. They observed that some teachers treated them like infants and did not like to be proved wrong about anything. It was suggested that younger teachers were more likely to negotiate issues with students compared with older teachers. As one student put it in discussion: 'If teachers and students were closer it would improve learning'. Dilon agreed with Laura concerning teacher education, arguing that teachers, like students, needed guidance on showing respect to all, regardless of age:

> They [teachers] would need to be taught how to respect one another, and that racism will not be tolerated and give punishments for racist incidents, so it don't carry on. The good things are that racism hardly happens in my school, as everyone learns to respect one another, and they know what the consequences are.

Chelsea also advocated some kind of teacher training:

> Try to do some teachers' day where [teachers] are made aware that the younger generation are different to them, and have different opinions.

Most of the students at Green Lane suggested that there was not much overt or interpersonal racism in schools, but schools could do more to provide for diverse groups, promote equality and respect for diversity. Interestingly, one student articulated this as a universal right for all regardless of background. The comment reflects an understanding of human rights and a degree of global awareness:

> Well, things should be fair in the first place. People should be a lot more aware of the world today and how it is simple humanity to show every person that they are equal.

Students at Green Lane were attempting to find solutions to a problem that students observed across the city; namely, that some teachers did not respect students and that their day-to-day practices were sometimes unjust. This was sometimes simply expressed in very general terms, as in 'School would be better for me if there were not teachers who dislike students'. However, in other cases, it was expressed as a matter of bias or discriminatory behaviour by particular teachers:

> Various teachers discriminate against students who share different beliefs, I find this disgusting.
> Female Indian 018, School C

> Teachers need to be fair to all students.
> Male Pakistani 158, School E

> It would help me to learn if teachers taught students equally not favour clever pupils.
> Female Indian 031, School A

> Give all students equal opportunities meaning more clever people won't get more opportunities.
> Female African Asian 007, School G

> If . . . everyone was treated fairly by teachers not matter what race.
> Female White and Asian 023, School C

> I think by being respected for who I am and what I am will make me a better student.
> Male Other Black African, 087, School D

> If . . . the teachers didn't prejudge me or anyone else.
> Female White and Asian 011, School C

> School would be much easier if you knew that your homework was marked equally like others other than thinking just because your [you're] Somalian your [you're] either trouble or dumb.
> Male Black Somali 2833, School G

There was recognition throughout of the reciprocal nature of understanding, respect and fairness for both teachers and students, as expressed by this student at School I: 'If teachers want respect they should give students respect too and they should also respect our ideas and our view' and:

> School would be a much more positive experience for me if . . . teachers gave students the same respect as I give them.
> Female Other Asian, Green Lane Community College

Often the difficulties were acknowledged to be part of a wider tension between young people and adults related to the status of young people in society:

> Students should not be seen as inferior to adults.
> Male Pakistani 013, School F

Students gave many examples of small ways in which teachers could demonstrate respect to students, such as not shouting, not pushing in in the lunch queue, not restricting rewards, such as school trips, to the highest attaining students, and most importantly, giving students a chance to put their case across, allowing them to disagree politely, and, above all, by listening.

Bullying and violence

Bullying is an issue about which all schools in England have been have been made aware. They are expected to develop anti-bullying policies that aim to protect students. Previous research into exclusion from school, including self-exclusion, highlighted that bullying was the only factor in school exclusion that students perceived differently from the professionals who worked with them. Whereas young people placed it high on the list of factors that might lead to exclusion, professionals were unlikely to make a causal link between bullying and exclusion from school or exclusion from learning (Osler and Vincent, 2003).

Young women also highlighted how forms of bullying experienced and practised by girls were much more difficult to detect than those practised or experienced by young men. These forms of bullying typically rely more heavily on psychological, rather than physical violence. Since this research was published, the use of technology, including mobile phones and the Internet, has made it easier for young people to practise forms of bullying that are unobserved by teachers, and consequently more difficult to detect or address. The issue of sexuality was raised just once in the survey. This is perhaps not surprising, since this kind of research tool does not lend itself easily to expressing concerns or identities that may not even be recognized as legitimate in some schools. The student simply wrote: 'School would be better for me if I could say I am gay'.

Across the city, students from all schools commented on how it would be easier to learn and to enjoy school if bullying was more effectively addressed. And while some students in discussion with the researchers suggested that racism was not a problem, in all schools there were students who expressed concerns about racism, sometimes linked to bullying. Sometimes students showed an awareness of general problems, not necessarily raising issues that they felt directly. As in the case of this white girl from school B:

> This school would be a better place if all the trouble makers and bullies were not here and there was no racism and discriminations and everyone was equal.

At school A there were calls for 'better anti-bullying policies', 'no racism' and the plea: 'If they were stricter with bullying, I might enjoy coming to school'. The call for 'better bullying programmes' was repeated at Long Meadow School. At Green Lane School, Selma (White European female) observed:

> I think the different year groups should come together because sometimes bullying is older people who don't really know the other. If you had people to talk to it would be easier to deal with and solve.

There appeared to be general agreement across all schools that bullying could not be completely eradicated, but that if students were involved in finding a solution, that solution was more likely to be effective in improving the everyday life of all. Sometimes, however, there was no solution offered, just a simple request, as in 'Give me a safer working environment', as requested at the all boys' school K. Clearly, some students felt extremely vulnerable, as in the case of a student at school B, who requested a means of reporting instances of bullying anonymously. Another student at the same school extended the problem of security to travel to and from school, saying he would feel safe and be able to learn more effectively 'if the area [around school] was much safer'.

At school G a number of issues were raised about the treatment of girls, by both teachers and boys at the school. For example, one girl asked for girls' 'rights on the [football] pitch' to be respected with opportunities for girls to play a wider range of sports. Another girl explained that she would feel safer at school if there were 'less perverted boys', suggesting a degree of sexual harassment. At a number of schools there were complaints about 'sexist teachers' although the problems were not elaborated. Boys also made occasional comments about gender inequalities in statements like: 'It's important for teachers to realise girls misbehave too' and for requests for 'equal punishments for both sexes'. This confirms the observations of girls in previous research who suggested they found it relatively easy to escape punishment on some occasions by using strategies like apologizing or crying, noting that boys did not find it easy to back down when in confrontation with teachers (Osler and Vincent, 2003).

Conclusion

Students did not simply identify injustices in school; many also tried to offer solutions to perceived problems. There were a number of suggestions from students about what schools needed to do more to promote diversity and equality. Students noted that racism should not be tolerated in schools: racist teachers should not be teaching; there should be punishments for racist incidents. They suggested that there needed to be more teaching about diversity (groups and cultures, celebrations and views), provision for diversity (religious requirements, i.e. halal food, dress, prayer rooms) and diversity in schools (having teachers from diverse backgrounds, equal treatment of all students). This is most clearly articulated in a discussion between students at Green Lane Community College about how schools should address diversity and ensure equality:

> There definitely [are] things that schools can do more for different ethnicities in schools but that also doesn't mean that there's much racism in all schools either. There's little things that could be done like halal food for Muslims.
>
> Sunita

They should be able to wear their religious dress. Provide more halal foods. Not much racism in school. Ask their views on things, such as PE with boys.

Kirandeep

Treat them the same in every way. Treat their celebrations seriously and maybe do some displays. Do food to suit every religion. When people need to pray, have rooms so at lunchtime they can go there.

Chelsea

Provide [for] the needs of different people and everyone should be treated equally. Racist people should be taken out.

Alim

Make sure racist people aren't employed and teach the students about religions and backgrounds other than theirs. Racism should be dealt with severely so it didn't keep happening.

Selma

Make sure that personal things like the [student's] background are kept personal. Teacher's should always treat the student equal to everyone, not throwing religion, race in their face. I don't think that racism can ever be stopped, apart from trying to make them understand, that different religions have different views.

Laura

Interestingly, in this discussion, it is the non-Muslim students who are suggesting how Muslim students' needs and religious practices can be accommodated through the provision of halal food and prayer rooms in school. These students are demonstrating tolerance and an understanding of diversity. They are also demonstrating that aspects of their education – at home or at school – have prepared them for living in contexts of diversity. They recognize the need for democratic dialogue: 'Ask them' and consult. They also recognize the need to persist in education for tolerance: 'Trying to make them understand that different religions (and cultures) have different views'. A strong learning dialogue needs to be developed in all schools between students and between teachers and students, so that education for democracy and diversity can be made more effective.

8 Children, participation and citizenship

This chapter explores the meaning of students' perspectives on schooling for schools, educational and social policy-makers and society. It is concerned with the implementation of children's rights and the practice of citizenship. It argues for a transformation in society's attitude to children and young people that requires, in turn, a transformation of schooling. The future health of democratic societies depends on a reworking of relationships between adults and young people in and beyond the school.

The evidence presented suggests that young people in this study are in many ways highly critical of their schooling. This raises a number of questions including:

1. Are these viewpoints typical of students more generally?
2. How can schools and education authorities meet their legal and moral duties to listen to young people and take due consideration of their perspectives in decision-making?
3. What structures and other arrangements are needed to listen to young people?
4. When we hear what young people have to say, what are we going to do?

It is one thing to know about young people's perspectives on schooling; it is another to *act* on these. It is clear from the evidence presented that while the young people have a range of concerns about their schooling, and many ideas for addressing particular problems, their biggest single concern is that they *do not have a say* in the decisions affecting them. This is the case whether decisions are about individuals; for example, when to involve an education social worker in a case where a young person has a poor record of attendance, or about wider issues affecting the whole student population, such as how the school budget is spent.

Knowing what is best for children

Adults often believe they know what is in the best interest of children, whether or not they have asked the children in question for their opinions.

Yet particular rights within the United Nations Convention on the Rights of the Child (CRC) cannot be taken in isolation. The best interest principle built into Article 3, which should be a consideration in decision-making, needs to be matched with the participation rights articulated elsewhere in the CRC, particularly that in Article 12.

Some adults may feel anxious that if they grant children and young people participation rights, they will take advantage of these rights to select options that are not in their long-term interests. In all cases children need to be provided with adequate information as well as guidance and support so they understand the implications of their decisions. Information and guidance are also among the rights guaranteed within the framework of the CRC (see Articles 13 and 5). A critical question to ask is: Will this choice *permanently* close down a particular future for the child or young person? (Feinberg, 1980; Freeman, 1988) Freeman is arguing for equal concern and respect for children, as for adults, but he warns against liberationists who place children's participation outside of any framework of protection. Protecting children involves protecting their rights. He stresses the duty to listen carefully to children, rather than make the assumption that they lack capacity or competence to think and act for themselves:

> We have to recognise the moral integrity of children, we have to treat them as persons entitled to equal concern and respect and entitled to have their autonomy and self-determination recognised. But children, particularly younger children, do need protection. We must not, as some liberationists would, 'abandon them to their rights'.
>
> (Freeman, 1988: 309)

So some decision-making might be best postponed by the younger child; there are also restrictions to protect children. But these should not automatically override children's participation rights or autonomy, or be used to deny children these rights. Children need to be able to make their decisions and express their opinions in contexts in which they enjoy appropriate guidance and support, but not unnecessary control. And there clearly are rights, such as freedom of conscience (Article 14) and freedom of association (Article 15), which mature young people will be in a position to exercise without need for consultation with adults.

Other adults may believe that it is important that children and young people have a say, but may not know what to do with their suggestions, especially in contexts like schools, where not all young people may be in agreement. Adult professionals may question whether such rights should be prioritized over what they identify as the core aspects of schooling; namely, teaching and learning. But children's rights cannot be ignored because they are administratively inconvenient. The evidence from this study is that young people believe their capacity to learn is inextricably linked to their sense of efficacy.

How should differences of opinion be accommodated? This issue is an important one, but it is no different from similar dilemmas concerning adult preferences. Not all adults will agree, but we usually manage to find ways of working together and living together in communities through a mixture of democratic participation, compromise and protection of the rights and interests of those who hold minority perspectives. The same principles should apply in schools as in countries that aspire to be democratic. Schools should work to promote, and therefore practise, the principles of democracy.

Typical or atypical views?

How can we evaluate what the young people in this study are saying? Are their experiences and perceptions of schooling shared by other young people? Although the material contexts of different schools vary, there are legitimate concerns about the degree to which we accord young people working conditions that fulfil the basic minimum standards we would accord adult workers. The evidence from young people, presented in Chapter 5, relating to material conditions, such as quality of classrooms, hygiene, temperature control, provision of food and water, but also to rules relating to accessing basic facilities like toilets, suggests that schools sometimes ride roughshod over young people's basic rights. Such school regimes show little regard for young people's dignity and respect.

Yet rules, regulations and political choices about spending priorities are made within a broader social and cultural context. It is this cultural context in which children and young people are treated as lesser citizens than adults and denied participation rights that needs to be addressed.

There is one concern that the young people in this study are expressing about which there is consistency across all schools and within all groupings of students: they feel that *they do not have a say*. In this respect the study confirms the claims of earlier research (Morrow, 1999). They are not asking to be the primacy decision-makers; merely to be involved in decision-making. Many explicitly acknowledge the expertise of their teachers, which they respect. They recognize that ultimate responsibility and decision-making lies with particular adults, whether these are teachers, education authorities or national government. All they are asking is that they are permitted to express a view; that they are supported in expressing their views; that due consideration is given to their perspectives; and that a system of decision-making exists, which permits adults to act on their views.

There are relatively few other studies where young people's perspectives of schooling are examined within a human rights framework. However, a study conducted on behalf of the Northern Ireland Commissioner for Children and Young People (NICCY) with children and young people in 27 schools did set out to evaluate law policy and practices that impact on children's lives in a number of domains and assess these against the standards in the CRC. The study investigated family life and alternative care; play and leisure; health; welfare and material deprivation; criminal justice and policy; as well as education (Kilkenny et al., 2004). In the NICCY study, as in the one reported in this book, children were concerned that they have very little say and no influence over decision-making.

Within the field of education, concerns about which children and young people in both locations felt they wanted a say and influence included: the state of the school buildings and facilities; recreation and sports opportunities, including school trips; teacher behaviour and levels of respect for young people; curriculum choices; and uniform. Children and young people in the two locations placed differing emphases on these various issues, but they were, nevertheless, common concerns.

There was one significant additional concern among the young people in the English multicultural city, which relates to respect for their religious beliefs and opportunities to celebrate non-Christian festivals. This issue also arose in Northern Ireland but its lack of prominence no doubt reflects the different demographic context, since there are in Northern Ireland proportionally fewer young people from non-Christian faith backgrounds.

Nevertheless, the need for the curriculum to specifically address issues of diversity and tolerance was a feature of both studies, related in the Northern Ireland context to continuing problems of sectarianism, where children grow up in a society where schools remain 'for all practical purposes, homogeneously Protestant or Catholic' (Kilkenny et al., 2004: 183). In these settings children continue to face in the post-conflict context the continuing impact of the conflict.

Some underlying problems identified in both studies are adult underestimation of the problem of bullying and the need for anti-bullying strategies that young people themselves buy into (Osler and Vincent, 2003) and the vulnerability of particular groups of young people, including Travellers; religious and ethnic minorities, young people with disabilities and lesbian, gay, transgender and bisexual (LGTB) young people. Each of the above issues has direct implications for the content and focus of teacher training and education. Additionally, as Kilkenny and her colleagues point out (2004: 183), there is a need to recognize the school as a 'site of child emotional abuse by teachers'. Many children experience extreme emotional violence and stress at school, a problem which, as Harber

(2004, 2008) identifies, is not peculiar to the UK or to one region of the world; it appears to be endemic.

Applying Article 12

Just as law, policy and practices in Northern Ireland were assessed against the standards of the CRC, so this also needs to happen in other jurisdictions. Of course, UN member states can draw on the observations and recommendations of the Committee on the Rights of the Child, as it relates to polices and practices within their territories, and this may help to establish some priorities for action, but the findings and reports of the Committee are no substitute for a full evaluation of the current standards in place and an action plan to ensure that children's participation rights, along with other rights, are addressed within formal legal and policy frameworks.

Schools and education authorities do not have to wait for governments to take the initiative in addressing children's participation rights in schooling. There are many steps they can take. And in guaranteeing children's participation rights, they will also be guaranteeing rights of provision and protection. Children who are equipped to participate and give their views, and who know those views will be listened to and given due weight, have greater confidence in voicing concerns. This makes them less likely to be victims of exploitation, deprivation or abuse. They will be able to think, feel and act like citizens in claiming their rights, and be in a better position to take on the roles and responsibilities of citizens.

Chapter 2 considered the implications of the CRC and particularly Article 12 (Appendix 1) for schooling. Article 12 provides us with a legal framework in which we have a duty to listen to young people's views and give them due consideration. As noted in Chapter 2, Laura Lundy (2007: 933) has identified four elements of a model (see p. 18), which can be used to ensure that children are in a position to be properly involved in educational decision-making. The model builds on both aspects of Article 12, the right to express a view and the right to have the view given due weight, identifying four key elements:

Space: children must be given the opportunity to express a view
Voice: children must be facilitated to express their views
Audience: the view must be listened to
Influence: the view must be acted upon, as appropriate.
(Lundy, 2007: 933)

There was a very strong desire to become involved constructively in the processes of decision-making among the students in this study, coupled with a real sense of frustration, as expressed in this comment:

> I would help the school with ideas but they never want the stu-
> dents' way...if the people would just listen, we could make a
> start.
>
> Male African Asian 056, School F

The evidence provided by the young people is now considered within the
framework of Lundy's model in order to understand barriers and opportunities that exist in supporting students' participation rights in schools. The
students' perspectives are examined in this way so as to inform the processes by which their voices, and the voices of other children and young
people, might be supported, heard, given due weight and acted upon by
adults working with them.

Expressing a view: space and voice

Space and encouragement

Article 12 makes clear the duty of schools and other bodies to 'assure' the
child a right to express their views and this implies the mechanism or
space by which this can be achieved. It is the school's responsibility to
ensure that the views of students are not simply heard when they choose
to express them, but that a space is provided and the views of students
actively sought. Key questions include: what school matters concern you?
Do you want to be involved in decision-making processes? If yes, how do
you feel we can most effectively involve you?

   This may imply a structure or channel through which children's opinions can be sought, and certainly some kind of regularization of the processes of consultation, so that schools and teachers are actively and rou-
tinely engaged in asking for children's opinions. One such space might
be a school or student council. However, a number of students expressed
the view that the school council did not work to seek their views, or that
it was only consulted on trivial matters; matters preselected by teachers;
or on issues that did not matter to them:

> Give us a voice not just some poxy little council which discusses
> how much the price of chips are.
>
> Male White British 020, School H

> [It would help] if we had a say in what goes on in school instead of
> having no actual important role in the school. Student councils
> are pointless and the teachers don't actually respect and encour-
> age our opinions, they try and force their own on us.
>
> Female White European 014, School H

It is also important that students see a transparent link between the space created to express their views and the processes by which these views are given due weight and acted upon. So, for example, there was the request from School J that the school council should be given 'more say' and that it should have a budget (and therefore power and influence) to ensure its decisions were implemented.

Communication channels need to be developed or, as one student at School D expressed it: 'Have students' views heard throughout the school'. Some of the requests sound like desperate pleas as in this request from School I: 'Listen to all our views, listen to all our ideas. Let us have more freedom and let us be treated more as an adult. We need independence'. Or this from School D: 'Please listen to our opinions. Let us have a say in the school'. Sometimes the point is expressed simply and succinctly: 'My opinion should be heard'.

This 'freedom to speak' was clearly related at least as much to the quality of relationships between teachers and students as to mechanisms. Some students felt they were actively discouraged from expressing an opinion:

> If [only] . . . the teachers would not use their authority to under-mine students.
>
> Female Pakistani, School B

> If students got a chance to voice their opinions with confidence [and] that teachers will not contradict them.
>
> Female White Black Caribbean 301, Long Meadow School

Alternatively, 'Listen to everyone's own opinion and if someone makes a point, listen don't correct them'; 'Listen when I have something to say'; 'Listen more carefully'. Teacher shouting is seen as a real barrier to self-expression and learning, as articulated at School G and elsewhere: 'School would be more enjoyable if [students could] ask questions without getting shouted at'.

A number of students feel there is active censorship of their viewpoints, and that this arises from teachers trying to exercise unreasonable control:

> Be able to say more of your own views, speak what's on your mind, without teachers saying to you, you can't say it.
>
> Female White British 004, School B

As Lundy notes, when discussing her model, there is a clear link between space and encouragement to speak and actually expressing a voice or having a voice.

Voice

The students in this study, aged 14–15, were less concerned with finding alternative means of expression, although a number who spoke English as an additional language did request more help with English. In particular cases, interpretation services might be necessary. The ability to express yourself and the claiming of voice are closely linked. Students often need motivating when there is an area of the curriculum in which they are less successful. The opportunity to express a voice about matters of importance to them might well provide academic motivation to many, giving an intrinsic purpose to learning, rather than the extrinsic goal that teachers emphasized: passing examinations. The argument can also be reversed: enabling students to become more articulate is likely to improve their chances of developing their voice. Some students felt that 'having a say' motivated them to succeed:

> I would do better, and so would others, if [students] had more of a say concerning matters of the school.
>
> Female Indian 258, School G

Younger students, in particular, may need drama, art and other imaginative aids to express a voice, as will some students with special educational needs. As was seen in Chapter 1, the play *Killing Mockingbirds: A 21st Century Field Guide* was a means through which young people aimed to open up a debate about key political and social issues that affected them both directly and indirectly. A few students had more radical suggestions about how power relationships in school might be transformed, such as this one from School E: 'Change the rules and allow [us] to vote for a student to run the school for a month'.

A deeper understanding of human rights and the meaning of 'freedom of expression' is also critical in developing a voice and ensuring it is heard. The students did not generally use this term, but it is a concept they need to understand and apply. It was occasionally used as in: 'Let students express their ideas freely, by letting us not wear uniform'.

Non-discrimination

Lundy's (2007) model also addresses non-discrimination (CRC, Article 2) which, of course, applies in the implementation of all rights. Non-discrimination is a key principle, both in the ways students treat each other, and in the ways in which teachers act. Bullying, peer pressure and discrimination were identified by some as a barrier to learning; it would seem to be an equal barrier to self-expression:

Students should respect other students for who and what they are and believe.
Female Pakistani 023, School B

In the minds of many students there was a link between what they referred to as 'equality' between teachers and students, justice, and having a voice:

If you complain about the teachers no action is actually taken. If a teacher complains about you, you always get a report, warning and a very big investigation. I have always wondered what has happened to equal rights?
Male African Asian 056, School F

At Long Meadow School, some saw the members of the school's student council who took part in our research workshop as an elite group who were consulted, while they were not. It is critical that there are means of ensuring that all students, especially the marginalized, are able to express their views.

Information

Article 13 of the CRC addresses the right to information and this is a key aspect of children's participation rights. Since a right cannot be claimed unless you know about it, this implies education in human rights. So the provision of human rights education (Article 29: 1b) is a key element in enabling them to claim participation rights.

Decision-making requires information. Sometimes children and young people are assumed to be incapable of making wide decisions simply because they lack information. Many young people felt that when they tried to express an opinion they were seen to be undermining adult authority. This implies more information also for teachers and a deeper understanding of children's rights, something that needs to be built into professional development, as well as initial teacher education.

What is clear from this study is that students have no difficulty identifying needs within the current context of schooling. Part of a process of drawing on children's' perspectives in school policy development would be a transformation from school as a place where adults believe they have all (or most) of the answers to one where they recognize children and young people also have the key to solving many problems.

Once such a culture change is in progress children and young people are in a stronger position to identity their own information needs, as well as to receive support in identifying these. So, just as they now say school would be a place where they could learn more if 'we had some say in the books we study', so they would become more competent in articulating their information needs to support their participation rights in such an environment. They already argue that 'Students should be able to explain ideas' and they would be more confident about the help they need in achieving this.

Giving due weight to views: audience and influence

Audience

The students voiced strongly a desire to be listened to. They generally felt equipped to express their views, although they identified barriers relating to structural means (e.g. inadequate school councils) or interpersonal relationships (teachers who did not support or encourage self-expression). But the challenge of persuading teachers to actively listen and give weight to their perspectives was presented as almost insurmountable in their accounts. One girl expressed it as follows:

> [It would help] if they [teachers] listened once in a while to our views instead of thinking they're always right. If teachers want respect they should give students respect too and they should also respect our ideas and our views.
>
> Female White Black 105, School H

This perception that teachers rarely listened was repeatedly made:

> I'd be in a stronger position to succeed if the teachers listen to us on what we've got to say regarding the content we are taught in lessons and the coursework that we do.
>
> Female Indian 258, School G

> It would be so much better if we could have our own opinions instead of the teachers saying 'yes, yes, we will think about that' and don't even do anything.
>
> Female White Black 007, School C

This perspective was echoed by other students: 'If only our opinions counted' was a variation on this refrain. Another student declared: 'Let everyone have a say, not just school council'. Students feel their autonomy and respect denied when teachers fail to engage with them before they take action:

> *Teachers should talk to students who they are worried about* and find out the main reason for missing school.
>
> Female African Asian 171, Long Meadow School (my emphasis)

If only teachers actually listened to my opinion.
Male Traveller, School F

My opinion should be heard out and [I should be able to] ask the questions without getting shouted at.
Male Indian 2580, School G.

Lundy (2007) suggests that teachers need to be trained in the skills of active listening. This might support better communication of students' ideas in some cases, but the problem runs deep and relates to the culture of schooling and the accepted norms of adult–student relationships within schools and to those of adult–young people relationships throughout society. It requires society to show children and young people equal respect and recognize their competence (Freeman, 1988), rather than assume incompetence.

Influence

Influence, in Lundy's (2007) model, refers to the 'due weight' to be given to the child's views. Audience and influence are closely interrelated in the processes by which young people's views are given due weight in decision-making. Students' lack of agency at school, concerning material conditions, rules, and the development of clear and trusted mechanisms by which they might change things, mean they express a degree of cynicism concerning their influence.

Many of the young people believed that they needed to be treated 'like adults' and by this they referred to respect for themselves and their views, but also to a degree of equity with adults in the provision of facilities. Since they spent all day at school, they needed comfortable, clean surroundings 'like teachers' where they could relax. They needed a degree of autonomy in their movement about the building and access to classrooms, toilets, the library and computers. That teachers failed to understand how they experienced school was a huge source of frustration: 'I wish teachers cared about your ideas. If only teachers accepted your ideas.' So poor material conditions that appear to be ignored, students' sense of powerlessness, and a widespread sense of frustration, all threaten to cloud the picture and may hinder adults from seeing students' potential. These factors limit opportunities for students to demonstrate their potential contribution. Even when students persuaded teachers to listen, they felt their opinions rarely counted:

I wish for once that student opinions would be heard *and something be done about it.*
Female Indian 032, Long Meadow School (my emphasis)

> If the teachers would listen to our opinions and ideas, take them into account, do something about the problems which concern us as students then we will be able to work more effectively and enjoy school a lot more.
>
> Male Pakistani 136, School D

At School G one student advised: 'Listen to student views before taking actions. School would be better if you make sure students had more rights.' While at School K, one suggested improvement was that students should be 'asked for [their] opinion about how to spend council grants or funds'.

Students need transparent processes by which they can understand how influence might be achieved. Although we, as researchers, were able to report to students how we were taking their ideas forward with schools, there was no clear feedback to us (and seemingly neither to students) on how their ideas were received.

There is growing evidence to support Alderson's (2000a) observation that ineffective or tokenistic school councils, for example, are more damaging to students' sense of efficacy and participation than having no council at all. Alderson (2000b: 130) concludes that the work of improving schools 'can only fully be achieved when adults work more equally with children as contributing citizens in democratic school communities'.

It is this challenge that some young people in this study also recognized. Consultation, in the sense proposed by Rudduck and Mcintyre (2007), seems inadequate when measured against this criterion. Lundy (2007) observes that discussions of Article 12 often assume that adults will always play some part in decision-making. She points out however that since Article 5, which identifies adults' right to provide appropriate direction and guidance, must be carried out in 'a manner consistent with the evolving capacities of the child', there will be contexts in which 'the adults' right to provide guidance wanes as the child matures and may eventually cease' (2007: 939). It is this scenario that adults in professional settings, including teachers, may find especially challenging. Not only does this imply that schools should be transformed, but that the wider society reconsiders adult–child relationships.

Society's (dis)trust of children

Interestingly, a plan by President Obama to broadcast directly to the nation's children at the start of the school year on 8 September 2009, and invite them to discuss 'notable quotes' from his speeches on education, attracted strong criticism from Republicans and other conservatives, who accused the president of indoctrination and using public money to promote his own ideology. This opposition was taking place in the context of fierce debates about President Obama's proposals for universal health care and it plays on fear and distrust of the president himself, but also reveals a deep distrust of children. Why should not children, who have direct experience of public schools, feed into a national policy debate on education?

The US Department of Education responded to criticism by stressing that students would not be encouraged to discuss education policy. Instead: 'The president will challenge students to work hard, set educational goals, and take responsibility for their learning'. The Presidential speech went ahead with this emphasis, and activities posted on the Department's website invited young children to consider:

- If you were the president, what would you tell students?
- What can students do to help in our schools?
- Why is it important that we listen to the president and other elected officials, like the mayor, senators, members of congress, or the governor? Why is what they say important?

Follow-up activities for young children include discussion of questions such as:

- What do you think the president wants us to do?
- Does the speech make you want to do anything?
- Are we able to do what President Obama is asking of us?
- What would you like to tell the president?

A degree of participation is encouraged among older students in the follow-up, with teachers leading a guided discussion covering:

> What resonated with you from President Obama's speech? What lines or phrases do you remember?
> Is President Obama inspiring you to do anything? Is he challenging you to do anything?
> What do you believe are the challenges of your generation?
> How can you be a part of addressing these challenges?
> (US Department of Education, 2009)

While teachers are certainly able to follow up such a speech in ways they choose, journalists note:

> It would seem that an opportunity to invite young people to engage in a broader policy debate about the future direction of education is too controversial.
> (*Los Angeles Times*, 2009)

> Opposition politicians claim that the young will be indoctrinated,
> but by doing so, distance them from the very debates about which
> they are likely to be able to make an important contribution, based
> on first-hand experience of schooling.
>
> (MacAskill, 2009: 19)

This proposal to engage young people in a policy debate is controversial, and apparently judged by some to be indoctrination. But the very charge of indoctrination reveals a deep-seated mistrust in some quarters, perhaps of teachers, certainly of Barrack Obama and his administration, but more interestingly in the context of this research, of children and young people themselves. How can a group of citizens in a mature democracy make the claim that to engage a group of fellow citizens in a policy debate will amount to indoctrination? The answer can only be that they believe (and/or assume many of their fellow citizens will believe) that children lack the maturity, insight and competence to take part. It is not worth engaging this group of (young) citizens in the debate, because they cannot be expected to speak with insight or authority about their own lives and experiences.

Pervasive paternalism

Some 40 years ago, Hillary Rodham (1973: 487) characterized children's rights as 'a slogan in search of a definition'. Although legal experts and policy-makers in a range of fields are now able to look to the CRC for an authoritative definition of children's rights, children and young people encounter a number of difficulties in claiming these rights. Not least of these is an all-pervading paternalistic culture and legal framework, which assumes that adults and, in particular parents, are best placed to assess children's needs, take decisions on their behalf, and secure their interests.

In many ways the situation of children at the beginning of the twenty-first century parallels that of women in Europe and elsewhere in the first decades of the twentieth century. Just as men (fathers, husbands, brothers, guardians) were regularly assumed to be in the best position to take major decisions on behalf of women during that era, without reference to the viewpoints or preferences of the individual concerned, so today adults (parents, teachers, health professionals, social workers) are often assumed to be best placed to take decisions that may determine the future life chances of children and young people, without due consideration of the views of the child in question.

In UK education law and policy, it is parents who enjoy rights and entitlements on behalf of their children. Faced with concerns from the

Committee on the Rights of the Child that children and young people in the UK lack mechanisms to ensure their participation in decision-making processes, and that they have no right of appeal against decisions made about them, there is a predictable response from government: these rights are vested in parents. So, for example, in the case of special needs tribunals or school exclusions, where there are no appeals procedures open to the child, officials point out that parents are able to exercise the right to appeal (Osler and Hill, 1999; Osler and Osler, 2002). They claim there are procedures whereby inappropriate or unjust decisions can be overturned. Education legal frameworks, they argue, do provide opportunities for democratic engagement and decision-making, although in reality children and young people are largely excluded from these.

Although, since the CRC was enacted, different UK governments have legislated to centralize and define the school curriculum in England, and have even gone so far as to prescribe teaching methods in the case of the literacy and numeracy hours in primary schools, when it comes to school governance and involving students in decisions about their schooling through mechanisms such as school councils, ministers revert to a neo-liberal discourse insisting that in these matters schools have the freedom to decide their own affairs (Davies and Kirkpatrick, 2000). Officials insist that within UK legal frameworks it is customary for parents to exercise these rights on behalf of children. Just because it is customary does not necessarily mean that young people's best interests are guaranteed through these procedures. Parents are not always best placed to protect the child's interests; sometimes the interests of parents and their children are in conflict.

Just as in the USA, conservative opponents of the CRC argue that it threatens to undermine the family so in the UK, conservative policy-makers insist that it is not necessary to review education law to bring it in line with the CRC, claiming that children's interests are adequately protected by laws that accord these rights to parents on behalf of their children. In a society where there are low levels of public awareness about human rights in general, and where children and their advocates have limited political influence, such claims may go unchallenged. Thus, conservative opponents of children's rights are confidently able to assert that no change is necessary, and in any case, children lack the emotional maturity or stability to make autonomous decisions.

If we substitute 'husbands and wives' for 'parents and children' in these claims, it becomes apparent that children as a category, like women during the era of the struggle for women's suffrage, are judged as somewhat incompetent citizens, whose interests are best represented by another class of citizens who are assumed to be uniformly rational, uniformly benevolent, and free from any conflicts of interest in maintaining the status quo. There is little discussion of power relations and no consideration of children's autonomy.

Critiques of human rights and children's rights

From the perspective of the political right, attention to children's rights undermines not just the authority of parents but also the freedom and autonomy of the family unit through unnecessary state intervention. Of course, expressed concerns about freedom and autonomy refer exclusively to the freedom and autonomy of adults, not children, who remain the most vulnerable members of society. Criticisms of children's rights from this perspective idealize the family, glossing over the violence and intimidation that many children experience. They overlook ongoing societal problems, including child poverty, domestic violence, and children's particular vulnerability to violence and abuse, which children's rights aim to address.

Communitarians have also attacked rights discourse, claiming that many of the problems of contemporary society can be attributed to a socio-cultural trend that emphasizes rights at the expense of responsibilities (Etzioni, 1995). Yet human rights require human solidarity, cooperation and reciprocity in order to work, and so it is not clear from these arguments how they promote irresponsibility. Unfortunately, these arguments, when applied to the young, tend to carry sway, since there is a tendency in many societies for young people to be characterized as irresponsible and thereby more likely than other groups to insist on claiming their rights without any consideration of the rights of others. This viewpoint has been shown to be prevalent in sections of the teaching profession (Carter and Osler, 2000; Hudson, 2005) yet teachers may be among those who also perceive that their own interests are threatened and their professional lives troubled by a child rights discourse.

Other critiques of rights and rights talk attempt to explain the gap between the ideals and the practice. These critiques question whether a focus on legal standards may detract from action to alleviate injustice. Rights are presented as abstractions and as symbolic statements over which legal experts argue, while the main causes of injustice, power differentials, self-interest and economic inequality go unchallenged. If we apply these considerations to children's rights and children's position in society, we can acknowledge that they are to a degree justified. Legal frameworks alone are inadequate. But as educators will recognize, legal frameworks need to be backed by awareness-raising and education in order for them to be effective, as the CRC acknowledges in Articles 29 (confirming children's right to human rights education) and 42, which places an obligation on signatories to make the principles and provisions of the Convention 'widely known'. This much is clear: a right is not an effective right unless you know about it.

But the critique of rights talk goes deeper than this. One suggestion is that that language of rights undermines real social progress, acting as a kind of smokescreen. A rights discourse detracts from the real goal, which is to bring about genuine social change. Rights are a diversion.

This argument stems in part from a misunderstanding of human rights. It presents rights as a vague and unhelpful diversion, whereas human rights are potentially strong indicators against which real social progress can be measured. Human rights are not vague standards; they can be used by oppressed groups as a means of holding the powerful, including governments, to account. Their universality means that a group experiencing an injustice in one jurisdiction can appeal to fellow humanity worldwide for solidarity. So, for example, by petition, an individual or group can challenge an injustice and require a government to bring about a change in domestic law that will protect others in the future. In this case the new cultural climate serves to prevent future injustices for the group. But the impact of the fight for justice may extend beyond the group in question or the jurisdiction in which they live. Others in distant places may be inspired to struggle for the same right.

Of course, there are weaknesses and limitations to existing human rights provisions. The CRC, for example, does not permit individual petition in the way that the European Convention on Human Rights (ECHR) does. Yet the CRC is not set in stone. It is a great, but flawed, achievement. There is ongoing discussion of how best to strengthen both the substance of the CRC and its implementation mechanisms. One means might be a protocol that would permit individual petition along the liens of that open to those seeking to claim their rights under the CRC. As Freeman (2000: 290) observes: 'The sight of children hauling their own states before an international court would be particularly gratifying'.

Human rights are not just about legal provisions. They are about standard setting and about using these international standards as part of a struggle for justice and equality before the law. Ultimately, they are about creating cultures where these legal provisions prevail. Just as a right is not an effective right unless you know about it (implying education and awareness-raising), so a right is not a right without struggle. The critique of rights that presents them as distractions and as a smokescreen fails to acknowledge how human rights have been used as part of the struggle of oppressed people in many different contexts. This is perhaps most famously illustrated in the case of the South African freedom struggle against apartheid. An appeal to universal human rights enabled the freedom fighters to cooperate with those who supported their cause but who were not part of the oppressed group, both within and beyond their nation's borders. Through the adoption of a human rights discourse, they were able to demonstrate the justice of their struggle and to secure the political benefits of solidarity with their fellow humanity against vested interests and powerful political enemies.

Children, violence and schooling

Perhaps the clearest example of children's vulnerability under English law lies in the threat of corporal punishment. While this was effectively outlawed in publicly funded schools in Britain in 1986, it remains lawful in the home under the defence of 'reasonable chastisement'. Children may still be beaten by parents in the name of family discipline. This is despite highly publicized campaigns by coalitions of children's advocacy organizations, such as 'Children are Unbeatable'. Although the CRC protects children against 'all forms of physical or mental violence, injury or abuse' (Article 19), many governments and human rights commissions, including that of the UK, choose to distinguish between what they characterize as corporal punishment (with an implement) and a 'safe smack'.

As Harber (2004) has demonstrated, schools across the globe remain authoritarian and often overtly violent institutions. Children remain subject to many forms of physical and mental violence, including peer bullying and corporal chastisement by teachers, even when this is explicitly outlawed. A number of countries, led by Sweden in 1979, have completely outlawed all forms of corporal punishment. This is a protection that is guaranteed for adults but does not yet extend to the world's children. The continuation of sanctioned violence against children and its tolerance in many societies demonstrates very vividly the gulf in status between children and adults as holders of human rights.

Children and citizenship in and beyond the school

The participation rights that are guaranteed to children and young people under the CRC effectively recognize them as citizens in the present, rather than citizens in waiting (Verhellen, 2000). Yet the CRC does not specify what rights the child should have in order to operate as a citizen (Freeman, 2000) and Van Bueren (1995: 141) has observed that under international law children are treated 'in a similar vein to aliens'.

Children and young people's perspectives and understanding of their own roles as citizens are not necessarily confined to the context of schooling. This section draws on qualitative data from research with children and young people in living in a West Coast metropolitan area of the USA, which explores their understandings of citizenship. It illustrates the capacity of children and young people to engage with complex political concepts and includes perspectives on schooling. It demonstrates that children and young people are also capable of understanding and engaging in wider political debates.

While Article 12 is often understood as the right of the child to contribute to decision-making relating *directly* to their own life, or to matters in which the child has a specific right, McGoldrick (1991: 141, quoted in Lundy, 2007) has pointed out that it applies much more widely, since a suggested amendment to this effect was not accepted during the drafting process.

The US study set out to explore children's and young people's perceptions of citizenship, and the ways in which they understood their own position and belonging as citizens within the nation and at other scales. The findings suggest that the young people in question have an interest in and awareness of national and international debates. Since Article 12 relates to the right to express views freely 'in all matters affecting the child', it seems important that these young citizens living in a democracy, who show an understanding of political debates, should have an opportunity of contributing to those debates that affect their lives less directly. Schools, and particularly lessons in citizenship and social studies, need to recognize young people's capacity for political thinking, which may often be underestimated, and to support them in their contributions to democratic dialogue.

In schools across the globe, despite a growing interest in global citizenship, education for citizenship is largely education for national citizenship. Perceived tensions exist between identification with local and cultural communities and the national community and between the nation and the global community. The young people in this small localized study were invited to reflect on different scales of belonging, from the school and their own neighbourhoods, through to the national and global.

Data gathering

The empirical data were gathered in 2007 from a workshop, run twice with a total of 30 fifth-graders (aged 10–11) and from group interviews with 10 high school students (aged 15–18) attending a leadership class. The fifth-grade students attended a private school, whereas the older students were attending a publicly funded school in an economically disadvantaged neighbourhood in the same city. Prior and subsequent to the workshops and interviews, the author had individual and group conversations with the elementary school principal, two of the three teachers whose classrooms were visited, and two adult volunteers working with the leadership class.

The contrasting schools were identified in collaboration with a US faculty colleague at the University of Washington. At the elementary school access was made through a direct approach to the principal, with a request to hold discussions with students on 'America's role in the world'. The precise terms of the data collection were then negotiated with the two class teachers whose students took part in the workshops.

The data collection methods in the elementary and high schools were selected to reflect the differing interests, ages and prior experiences of the students. The data were collected in a way that is designed to reflect the principles underpinning Article 12 of the CRC, which confirms the right of children to express their views freely 'in all matters affecting the child', and for these views be 'given due weight' in educational and other decision-making. The workshops for fifth-graders were structured so that every child would have an opportunity to contribute to a whole class discussion, a small group discussion, and a short group-based text, as well as record their own personal views.

Fourteen students participated in the first and sixteen in the second workshop. The students were arranged in small groups with a class teacher present for both workshops. The author introduced herself to students herself as a university teacher from England doing research at the University of Washington and explained she was interested in understanding children's and young people's perspectives. The particular focus of the session was how the students understood their own communities, America and the wider world. The students knew the researcher had already visited a high school on a number of occasions to collect data from older students as part of the same project.

Each student then introduced themselves by name with one thing about them that might help the researcher remember them. Everyone then completed the first two sections of an individual record entitled: 'Who am I?' (name, how I got this name and/or its meaning) and 'Where am I Coming From?' (information about people and places which have influenced me; my community; and my city).

Students then examined the first piece of stimulus material consisting of four pictures: the American flag; a 1940s poster of a man holding the flag; the Statue of Liberty; and a mime artist in a Paris park posing as the Statue of Liberty. The author invited the whole class to examine the text of the poster: 'This is Our Flag. We will decide what it means and how it will be used. Not you.' Students were asked to consider who 'we' and 'us' might be and who 'you' might be. Following a brief class discussion, the smaller groups then were invited to discuss what each of the four pictures represented to them and then to record their personal ideas in an individual piece of writing about these representations entitled: 'What America means to me'.

Finally, students were given a photograph of Langston Hughes, the Harlem Renaissance poet, together with the opening lines from his poem, Let America be America Again:

Let America be America again.
Let it be the dream it used to be.
Let it be the pioneer on the plain
Seeking a home where he himself is free.

(America never was America to me.)

Let America be the dream the dreamers dreamed–
(Langston Hughes [1938], 1994)

After reading these lines, the students were invited to say whether they thought Langston Hughes liked America or not. Opinions were divided; some thought he did, others thought he did not, since he wanted it to be different. After some discussion both the workshop groups arrived at a consensus that Langston Hughes liked America but he did not like some of the things that were happening at the time he wrote the poem. He wanted the country to change. The students put forward some ideas on what he might not have liked and then they engaged in the final group task:

What is America to us?
What do we like about America?
What don't we like?
What would we like to change?

These ideas were debated in the larger group, and then in small groups, where the students discussed them in more depth and recorded the group's ideas on their group record under the heading: 'What is America to us?' Finally, they recorded their individual ideas about what they liked, disliked and/or wanted to change about America on personal record sheets, under the heading: 'What does America mean to me?'

At the high school, focus group interviews were conducted with volunteers drawn from a leadership class, made up of young people aged 15–18, in their final three years of high school. The class consisted of students who had opted for this programme, augmented by students who had been ejected from other classes. Consequently, not all were committed to the goals of the class, which focused on making improvements to the school. The author observed the class on three occasions when they were planning a range of practical projects, such as setting up a school store. One of these sessions was led by a small team from the Equity and Race Relations section of the local school district and the theme was student voice and participation.

There were a number of opportunities for informal interaction with students before the focus group interviews. Two focus group interviews took place with a total of 10 students, with some students attending both sessions. On the first occasion the teachers and volunteers were present in the room working with other students. On the second occasion no other adults were present.

As with the younger students, the author explained her interest in learning about young people's perspectives. At the high school students were invited to talk about their experiences of schooling as well as their views on their local communities, citizenship and the nation. The students were promised that they and their school would not be identifiable in any future research report. They were particularly concerned that no one would be able to identify their school since they wanted to be critical, but were sensitive about its reputation.

The processes of data collection through the workshops and focus group interviews were underpinned by the principles of the CRC, and particularly by Article 12. Although the USA is one of just two countries worldwide that have not ratified the CRC, it represents a universal standard and the consensus of the international community on children's human rights. In applying the principles of the CRC to the research, the aim was to explore how children and young people's perspectives might inform schooling. The goal was to explore a concept of children's right to be heard in school that extends beyond the current interest in 'the voice of the child' or 'student voice', which can be tokenistic and may have little impact on policy and practice in education (Osler, 2006).

Although in the USA a failure to ratify the CRC means that there is no legal obligation to uphold children's rights as defined in the CRC, it is worth recalling that under Articles 12–16 children have the right to express an opinion; freedom of expression; freedom of thought, conscience and religion; freedom of association; and protection of privacy. These are all rights guaranteed in the Universal Declaration of Human Rights, 1948. The CRC reasserts that these rights apply to children as well as to adults.

The perspectives of students are presented here, examining their perspectives as members of a community, a city, and a nation.

My community

For the younger children, aged 10–11, and all drawn from privileged backgrounds, the concept of community was one linked first and foremost with a particular neighbourhood, but also with sports and other leisure activities:

I live in (neighbourhood] and there is a community center and it lets you do a bunch of sports.

Melina

I play in a soccer club called Crossfire.

Emmeline

My community is my fishing partners, and my soccer team.

Alex

Occasionally, the students linked community explicitly to a community spirit, as in team work, and cooperation:

My soccer team works together to win.

Keshav

But community was also linked to people, usually friends, but occasionally to an ethnic or cultural identity. Sometimes this was a community tied to a specific location; at other times not:

My community is my neighbors, my class and my friends outside of school.

Paloma

I am from a community that is a community of many people.

Alice

My community, it's a neighborhood with a lot of old people.

Edie

I live in [neighbourhood] with a lot of Jewish people. I am part Jewish so I fit in.

Josephine

And, finally, community was defined in terms of home and/or family:

I live on a houseboat witch [sic] is a house that floats on the water.

Finlay

The older students, from a school in a disadvantaged neighbourhood, spoke about their own neighbourhoods, and some of the challenges that they faced. These included: managing paid work and school (some worked for 30 hours a week or more); family responsibilities; and concerns about gangs and personal safety. Of the students, all of whom were girls, about half carried responsibilities for younger siblings. One student, who lived with both parents, explained that her parents' shift work patterns meant that she had primary responsibility for the younger children for up to three days at a time.

My city

In defining their city, the young children, most of whom were born in the USA, tended to name the city in which they all lived, which was variously described as nice, wet (referring to the weather), with lots of trees, full (meaning with a large population) and democratic. Other students chose the city (or sometimes the state) in which they were born; others the city of a parent's birth, particularly if this was from another country they had visited, so that students chose cities in Japan, Korea and Canada, and one chose Paris because she enjoyed the excellent shopping.

When asked about the city, the high school students talked about their part-time jobs, working in shops, for example, or being a member of a consumer panel at local department store where, in return for providing feedback on new fashion lines, two students received training in fashion and buying as well as pay. It was first and foremost as consumers or workers that they appeared to identify with the wider city.

The flag and the Statue of Liberty

In explaining the associations that they made with the flag and with the Statue of Liberty, the young students were aware they were talking to an outsider, to a foreigner, and so took care to explain their ideas very carefully. A few students began by explaining what they had clearly learned from textbooks: 'The American flag represents America, the fifty states, the first 13 colonies'. A few even checked the image of the flag the researcher gave them, counting the stars, to make sure she had not tricked them with a counterfeit. Some students explained that the flag was associated with New York and with 9/11, which was a very long way away. This felt like the reassurance that they might have been given in the immediate aftermath of 9/11 when they were just 4 or 5 years old. Some offered the explanation that flying the flag meant you loved America but that you also liked George Bush; a position they were uniformly keen to distance themselves from. Others suggested the flag represented a united country; one which was independent of other countries, and 'not controlled by some other place'. A number of students affirmed the flag was a symbol of freedom, but one asserted that it reflected 'war, evolution, domination, liberty' over past centuries and which continued to the present day.

The image on the poster they examined was of a blond man holding the flag, and dressed in working clothes dating from the 1940s. The poster's slogan read: 'This is Our Flag. We will decide what it means and how it will be used. Not you.' There were two broad interpretations of this. The first viewpoint was that 'we' were the people and 'you' the government. The poster represented the people and their 'freedom against government'.

Here, the concepts they were addressing were freedom and democracy, which in the minds of some children were synonyms. They explained that: 'They [the government] don't rule us! We rule them. They help us but don't rule us like a king. It is our opinion that counts.'

Other students suggested that 'we' and 'you' were Americans and foreigners. The slogan was addressed to foreigners: 'You can run your country your way but we rule ours our way. Not one person decides what to do, everyone does.' One child explained: 'Everyone chooses the flag not a single [person]. It is everyone's flag not one's.' Since the flag belonged to everyone, no one individual could claim it for themselves. It meant people had to discuss things and work out what they were going to do together. The flag also meant to another student: 'Spirit, patriotism, freedom of our country, you can't take it!' Or as another student expressed simply: 'This is our flag: not yours, not mine, it's ours. You will not decide what it means. We will all together decide what it means.' Others suggested that the poster was directed to the wider global community: 'It's telling the world it's our country. We were in war and some countries tried to take over.' 'It's about pride.' The message was interpreted as a warning to nations that might threaten America.

The students explained that the Statue of Liberty was symbolic of the USA, but was different from the flag in that it highlighted international solidarity:

- The Statue of Liberty represents a bond between the French and America. It also represents our freedom.
- It's a famous landmark in New York. It reminds us of France because the French made it.
- It means we have a special trust with the French.
- It's there to welcome people to a free land. It's a symbol of freedom.
- It represents eternal spirit, seven continents, liberty, and environmentalism. The Statue of Liberty means freedom for ever.

The children were intrigued by the mime artist posing as the Statue of Liberty and one or two were upset that a human statue might catch you out by moving! One suggested that its human size reminded us that every human being was free. Another suggested that it would encourage us to smile and that people should look up to the statue and love it. It was a reminder 'that freedom was everywhere' and that 'money-making, employment, comedy, and liberty were everywhere'.

What is America to me?

The children tended to associate America, first and foremost, both with ideals and as their 'home'. Concern and respect for the natural

environment also ran through their descriptions. The ideals they highlighted were generally linked to democracy and liberty, which they interpreted in different ways and which they were able to distinguish, in some
cases, as ideals rather than political realities:

- To me America is freedom, but is polluted and sad, most of all it
  is home.
- We like the wildlife and freedom.
- I love America.
- America means freedom, the environment and choices.
- America to me means less violence and a land of beauty.
- America is freedom and a land of beauty.
- The country where people can do what they want and feel good
  about it.
- America means freedom, war, good education.

What was particularly striking were the things that individuals wished
to change about America. Of most concern were the president (at that
time George Bush) and the war in Iraq. Some students made a point of
saying something positive about their country when they made a critical
comment about politics:

- I would love to change the political things, but I love the beauty
  that we have.
- America means home to us. The thing I would like to change is
  that we should stop this terrible war.

It was interesting that when they shared their ideas about change in small
groups, they started to propose policy changes:

- The thing we would like to change is that we should let the Mex-
  icans into our country and not send them back.
- We'd like to improve America, so that there is peace, more freedom, improve natural beauty, change the president, less fast food
  places/keep fast-food (debating) [i.e. there was no final agreement
  on this within the group], stop polluting, good community, less
  violence, less poverty, more appreciation [respect between people].

We want to change:

- president/government;
- pollution;
- cutting and destroying wildlife;
- war;
- we don't like global warming.

The younger students demonstrated that they were aware of a number of political issues and that they had an interest in and observations about contemporary politics. The teacher who observed the sessions commented that she had not realized how interested they were, or the extent of their knowledge, although when they were in the middle of discussion about the strengths and weaknesses of the president (Bush) and his policies, she chided one group, saying: 'We are not here to discuss politics. This is social studies.' They were patriotic but also critical of their government's policies at home and internationally. Many observed how much they 'loved America'. By contrast, the older, less privileged students insisted that being an American simply means 'You have a social security number'; 'You are not an immigrant, so you can get the minimum wage'. Seven of the ten students were themselves immigrants, and an eighth had been born to immigrant parents soon after their arrival in the USA.

The older students discussed the importance of education and explained that one of the reasons their parents had come to America was for a better life and particularly for better educational opportunities for their children. They were conscious, however, that their school had low status and that they had 'mostly old teachers' who 'don't want to move' and felt that expectations of them were low. They were also conscious that other schools were better funded and spoke of their own poverty and the pressures this brought to bear on family life, particularly the long hours their parents needed to work to make a living.

Although they chose not to identify with the nation, they did identify with their school (in spite of the criticisms made) and with their local neighbourhoods. Many of them also identified with their parents' country of origin, and among those who were American-born, with the state or city their parents had grown up in.

Participating in wider debates

The research suggests that young people of vastly different backgrounds and from quite a young age are interested in wider political issues and are ready to express an opinion. The teacher of the younger students said she had never heard them talk about such matters before. The older students reported they had not had such discussions before with an adult in school but that they did discuss many of these issues among themselves and with family members.

The younger students had cosmopolitan outlooks and many were concerned about poverty in their own city, about war, about people in other countries, and about America's role in the world. They identified strongly with their country, but their patriotism was of a critical kind. The older students did not share the younger ones 'love' of America, and identified first and foremost with the smaller communities of school and neighbourhood. They too were conscious of injustice and poverty, in their own lives, in the city and globally. They expressed concern about parents' hours of work, challenges in realizing their educational goals, and family difficulties relating to health care. They too were developing cosmopolitans, but with greater scepticism, as might be expected with greater maturity and exposure to hardship.

Evidence is emerging that young people do not necessarily identify primarily or exclusively with the nation state, but have flexible and shifting identities (Osler and Starkey 2003; Mitchell and Parker 2008). This is not something for politicians to fear, but for educators to build upon. The CRC recognizes children and young people as citizens in the present, not citizens-in-waiting, and makes explicit their participation rights. In working to implement Article 12, it is clear that many young people will wish to express their views about a wide range of matters affecting them, not just those relating to schools. The challenge facing schools and teachers is to offer appropriate support and information, so that young people's views will be given due consideration, alongside those of adults, whether the topic under consideration is the everyday processes of schooling, education policy or wider political issues.

9   Epilogue

This closing chapter returns to the play *Killing Mockingbirds: A 21st Century Field Guide*. A scene from this play, transcribed in Chapter 1, revealed how a group of student actors from two contrasting Seattle high schools identified immigrants to the USA as one group of today's mockingbirds; persons who are both invisible to and scapegoated by society, working, often without papers and fair wages, to support those from the mainstream. These immigrants are supporting the lifestyles of the rich and privileged, many of whom, as the students highlight, show a degree of hypocrisy in speaking out against undocumented immigrants while continuing to employ them. The scene also reminded the audience of their nation's story, which is built on a long history of economic migration; of people who helped develop the country while trying to make a better life for themselves and their families; and which includes the forced migration of African slaves as a source of labour and wealth creation.

In Chapter 8 we saw how children and young people, some as young as 10 years of age, are expressing their concerns about immigration policy; war; environmental damage; poverty; and injustice. Many of them are able to identify a number of contradictions between democratic ideals and everyday political realities.

Throughout this book, British students' perspectives have highlighted deeply entrenched problems in schooling. Students want to have a say in their lives at school, yet they seem to be near invisible when it comes to engagement in decision-making processes, even when these directly affect their own lives. They reveal a picture of their material conditions that legally protected adult employees would never tolerate, yet society allows children and young people to be treated in this way.

Not only do young people want a say in their own schooling; they have this right, under the UN Convention on the Rights of the Child (CRC), Article 12, to express their views freely 'in all matters affecting' them and for these views to be 'given due weight' in decision-making processes. The student actors in *Killing Mockingbirds* perceive young people as another group of today's mockingbirds; invisible and scapegoated. No doubt from the evidence presented here, they would see parallels between their lives and those of their British peers. This evidence reveals these British young people to be another group of mockingbirds.

Many adults in both countries continue to mistrust children and young people, and do not accept them as fellow citizens, ready and willing to contribute to policy debates; whether these are about education, on which they can draw directly on their experience, or on wider political issues that affect all of us. In fact, young people may have insights that reveal adult self-deception as the performance of *Killing Mockingbirds: A 21st Century Field Guide* revealed.

At the end of the performance, the students were joined on stage by Leticia Lopez, who had directed them, for an audience discussion. Audience members, who included many of the cast's family members, were hugely enthusiastic; they admired the actors' energy and appeared sympathetic to the play's concern for immigrants, the homeless and young people.

Then Leticia asked the actors, from both Roosevelt and Cleveland High Schools, what they had learned from working with each other in the Rough Eagles project. Students from both schools spoke warmly about the new friendships they had made. A Roosevelt student pointed out how membership of the project had challenged her stereotypes about the young people from the south side neighbourhood, about the neighbourhood itself, and the school. Another Roosevelt student noted how 'we are all the same' and that everyone, regardless of where they are from or what school they go to, can achieve great things together. The audience responded warmly and enthusiastically.

Then Leticia asked one particular young man from Cleveland High School whether he agreed. He responded carefully and thoughtfully. Yes, he had benefited from the project. Yes, he had proved to himself that he could be a successful part of an impressive team. Leticia pushed him further: did he believe that, at Cleveland, he could enjoy the same educational benefits as the students at Roosevelt? Yes, he could do well at school, and Cleveland High School had recently been refurbished; despite this, his school continued to lack some of the facilities at Roosevelt. He hesitated for a moment, this was not everything. He had also learned that Roosevelt students had something he did not have, even if he was to transfer to their school and study there. They had networks of support that he could not access. Right from the beginning, they had something that could not be found at school. They met people who helped them by putting opportunities their way. They could get experiences and advice that put them in a strong position to get the college place they wanted and the best jobs. They were learning things out of school that would stand them in good stead, whereas he was merely working in a part-time job to keep himself at school. This was what he had learned.

The audience was suddenly quiet and uncomfortable. This was not a message most wanted to hear. These adults know that different schools offer different educational opportunities. Importantly, they know funding is very uneven. Some schools manage on a basic budget, while others in more prosperous neighbourhoods attract significant additional financial support from students' families. But they do not want reminding of this. They understood too the point the Cleveland student was making about social capital. Again, this is a sensitive issue, which is easier to ignore than to discuss. Those who have set up their own children to succeed do not want to believe anything other than that in the USA anyone can succeed, if they put in the hard work.

Just as it was difficult for some adults in the *Killing Mockingbirds* audience to hear the perspective of this young man and to confront complex inequalities, so it remains difficult for many adults, perhaps especially education professionals, to listen to children and young people and respond to their realities.

Human rights belong to us all, and participation rights belong to children, as well as adults. Rights need to be known about in order for individuals and groups to be in a position to claim their rights, and children have an entitlement to education in human rights. But this is unlikely to be sufficient and realizing children's rights in schools is unlikely to be an easy or comfortable experience. Rights are rarely realized without a struggle. Children and young people need adults, whether they are teachers, school administrators, policy-makers or researchers, to work with them in a spirit of solidarity to help them transform schools into places where children's rights for all are no longer an ideal but a political reality for all children, including the marginalized.

Appendix: UN Convention on the Rights of the Child

Adopted and opened for signature, ratification and accession
by UN General Assembly resolution 44/25 of 20 November 1989
Entry into force 2 September 1990, in accordance with article
49

Preamble

The States Parties to the present Convention,

Considering that, in accordance with the principles proclaimed in the
Charter of the United Nations, recognition of the inherent dignity and of
the equal and inalienable rights of all members of the human family is
the foundation of freedom, justice and peace in the world,

Bearing in mind that the peoples of the United Nations have, in the
Charter, reaffirmed their faith in fundamental human rights and in the
dignity and worth of the human person, and have determined to promote
social progress and better standards of life in larger freedom,

Recognizing that the United Nations has, in the Universal Declaration
of Human Rights and in the International Covenants on Human Rights,
proclaimed and agreed that everyone is entitled to all the rights and freedoms set forth therein, without distinction of any kind, such as race,
colour, sex, language, religion, political or other opinion, national or social origin, property, birth or other status,

Recalling that, in the Universal Declaration of Human Rights, the
United Nations has proclaimed that childhood is entitled to special care
and assistance,

Convinced that the family, as the fundamental group of society and
the natural environment for the growth and well-being of all its members
and particularly children, should be afforded the necessary protection and
assistance so that it can fully assume its responsibilities within the community,

Recognizing that the child, for the full and harmonious development
of his or her personality, should grow up in a family environment, in an
atmosphere of happiness, love and understanding,

Considering that the child should be fully prepared to live an individual life in society, and brought up in the spirit of the ideals proclaimed in the Charter of the United Nations, and in particular in the spirit of peace, dignity, tolerance, freedom, equality and solidarity,

Bearing in mind that the need to extend particular care to the child has been stated in the Geneva Declaration of the Rights of the Child of 1924 and in the Declaration of the Rights of the Child adopted by the General Assembly on 20 November 1959 and recognized in the Universal Declaration of Human Rights, in the International Covenant on Civil and Political Rights (in particular in articles 23 and 24), in the International Covenant on Economic, Social and Cultural Rights (in particular in article 10) and in the statutes and relevant instruments of specialized agencies and international organizations concerned with the welfare of children,

Bearing in mind that, as indicated in the Declaration of the Rights of the Child, 'the child, by reason of his physical and mental immaturity, needs special safeguards and care, including appropriate legal protection, before as well as after birth',

Recalling the provisions of the Declaration on Social and Legal Principles relating to the Protection and Welfare of Children, with Special Reference to Foster Placement and Adoption Nationally and Internationally; the United Nations Standard Minimum Rules for the Administration of Juvenile Justice (The Beijing Rules); and the Declaration on the Protection of Women and Children in Emergency and Armed Conflict,

Recognizing that, in all countries in the world, there are children living in exceptionally difficult conditions, and that such children need special consideration,

Taking due account of the importance of the traditions and cultural values of each people for the protection and harmonious development of the child,

Recognizing the importance of international co-operation for improving the living conditions of children in every country, in particular in the developing countries,

Have agreed as follows:

PART I

Article 1

For the purposes of the present Convention, a child means every human being below the age of eighteen years unless under the law applicable to the child, majority is attained earlier.

Article 2

1. States Parties shall respect and ensure the rights set forth in the present Convention to each child within their jurisdiction without discrimination of any kind, irrespective of the child's or his or her parent's or legal guardian's race, colour, sex, language, religion, political or other opinion, national, ethnic or social origin, property, disability, birth or other status.
2. States Parties shall take all appropriate measures to ensure that the child is protected against all forms of discrimination or punishment on the basis of the status, activities, expressed opinions, or beliefs of the child's parents, legal guardians, or family members.

Article 3

1. In all actions concerning children, whether undertaken by public or private social welfare institutions, courts of law, administrative authorities or legislative bodies, the best interests of the child shall be a primary consideration.
2. States Parties undertake to ensure the child such protection and care as is necessary for his or her well-being, taking into account the rights and duties of his or her parents, legal guardians, or other individuals legally responsible for him or her, and, to this end, shall take all appropriate legislative and administrative measures.
3. States Parties shall ensure that the institutions, services and facilities responsible for the care or protection of children shall conform with the standards established by competent authorities, particularly in the areas of safety, health, in the number and suitability of their staff, as well as competent supervision.

Article 4

States Parties shall undertake all appropriate legislative, administrative, and other measures for the implementation of the rights recognized in the present Convention. With regard to economic, social and cultural rights, States Parties shall undertake such measures to the maximum extent of their available resources and, where needed, within the framework of international co-operation.

Article 5

States Parties shall respect the responsibilities, rights and duties of parents or, where applicable, the members of the extended family or community as provided for by local custom, legal guardians or other persons legally responsible for the child, to provide, in a manner consistent with the evolving capacities of the child, appropriate direction and guidance in the exercise by the child of the rights recognized in the present Convention.

Article 6

1. States Parties recognize that every child has the inherent right to life.
2. States Parties shall ensure to the maximum extent possible the survival and development of the child.

Article 7

1. The child shall be registered immediately after birth and shall have the right from birth to a name, the right to acquire a nationality and as far as possible, the right to know and be cared for by his or her parents.
2. States Parties shall ensure the implementation of these rights in accordance with their national law and their obligations under the relevant international instruments in this field, in particular where the child would otherwise be stateless.

Article 8

1. States Parties undertake to respect the right of the child to preserve his or her identity, including nationality, name and family relations as recognized by law without unlawful interference.
2. Where a child is illegally deprived of some or all of the elements of his or her identity, States Parties shall provide appropriate assistance and protection, with a view to re-establishing speedily his or her identity.

Article 9

1. States Parties shall ensure that a child shall not be separated from his or her parents against their will, except when competent authorities subject to judicial review determine, in accordance with applicable law and procedures, that such separation is necessary for the best interests of the child. Such determination may be necessary in a particular case such as one involving abuse or neglect of the child by the parents, or one where the parents are living separately and a decision must be made as to the child's place of residence.

2. In any proceedings pursuant to paragraph 1 of the present article, all interested parties shall be given an opportunity to participate in the proceedings and make their views known.

3. States Parties shall respect the right of the child who is separated from one or both parents to maintain personal relations and direct contact with both parents on a regular basis, except if it is contrary to the child's best interests.

4. Where such separation results from any action initiated by a State Party, such as the detention, imprisonment, exile, deportation or death (including death arising from any cause while the person is in the custody of the State) of one or both parents or of the child, that State Party shall, upon request, provide the parents, the child or, if appropriate, another member of the family with the essential information concerning the whereabouts of the absent member(s) of the family unless the provision of the information would be detrimental to the well-being of the child. States Parties shall further ensure that the submission of such a request shall of itself entail no adverse consequences for the person(s) concerned.

Article 10

1. In accordance with the obligation of States Parties under article 9, paragraph 1, applications by a child or his or her parents to enter or leave a State Party for the purpose of family reunification shall be dealt with by States Parties in a positive, humane and expeditious manner. States Parties shall further ensure that the submission of such a request shall entail no adverse consequences for the applicants and for the members of their family.

2. A child whose parents reside in different States shall have the right to maintain on a regular basis, save in exceptional circumstances personal relations and direct contacts with both parents. Towards

that end and in accordance with the obligation of States Parties under article 9, paragraph 1, States Parties shall respect the right of the child and his or her parents to leave any country, including their own, and to enter their own country. The right to leave any country shall be subject only to such restrictions as are prescribed by law and which are necessary to protect the national security, public order (ordre public), public health or morals or the rights and freedoms of others and are consistent with the other rights recognized in the present Convention.

Article 11

1. States Parties shall take measures to combat the illicit transfer and non-return of children abroad.
2. To this end, States Parties shall promote the conclusion of bilateral or multilateral agreements or accession to existing agreements.

Article 12

1. States Parties shall assure to the child who is capable of forming his or her own views the right to express those views freely in all matters affecting the child, the views of the child being given due weight in accordance with the age and maturity of the child.
2. For this purpose, the child shall in particular be provided the opportunity to be heard in any judicial and administrative proceedings affecting the child, either directly, or through a representative or an appropriate body, in a manner consistent with the procedural rules of national law.

Article 13

1. The child shall have the right to freedom of expression; this right shall include freedom to seek, receive and impart information and ideas of all kinds, regardless of frontiers, either orally, in writing or in print, in the form of art, or through any other media of the child's choice.
2. The exercise of this right may be subject to certain restrictions, but these shall only be such as are provided by law and are necessary:
    (a) For respect of the rights or reputations of others; or
    (b) For the protection of national security or of public order (ordre public), or of public health or morals.

Article 14

1. States Parties shall respect the right of the child to freedom of thought, conscience and religion.
2. States Parties shall respect the rights and duties of the parents and, when applicable, legal guardians, to provide direction to the child in the exercise of his or her right in a manner consistent with the evolving capacities of the child.
3. Freedom to manifest one's religion or beliefs may be subject only to such limitations as are prescribed by law and are necessary to protect public safety, order, health or morals, or the fundamental rights and freedoms of others.

Article 15

1. States Parties recognize the rights of the child to freedom of association and to freedom of peaceful assembly.
2. No restrictions may be placed on the exercise of these rights other than those imposed in conformity with the law and which are necessary in a democratic society in the interests of national security or public safety, public order (ordre public), the protection of public health or morals or the protection of the rights and freedoms of others.

Article 16

1. No child shall be subjected to arbitrary or unlawful interference with his or her privacy, family, or correspondence, nor to unlawful attacks on his or her honour and reputation.
2. The child has the right to the protection of the law against such interference or attacks.

Article 17

States Parties recognize the important function performed by the mass media and shall ensure that the child has access to information and material from a diversity of national and international sources, especially those aimed at the promotion of his or her social, spiritual and moral well-being and physical and mental health.

To this end, States Parties shall:

(a) Encourage the mass media to disseminate information and material of social and cultural benefit to the child and in accordance with the spirit of article 29;
(b) Encourage international co-operation in the production, exchange and dissemination of such information and material from a diversity of cultural, national and international sources;
(c) Encourage the production and dissemination of children's books;
(d) Encourage the mass media to have particular regard to the linguistic needs of the child who belongs to a minority group or who is indigenous;
(e) Encourage the development of appropriate guidelines for the protection of the child from information and material injurious to his or her well-being, bearing in mind the provisions of articles 13 and 18.

Article 18

1. States Parties shall use their best efforts to ensure recognition of the principle that both parents have common responsibilities for the upbringing and development of the child. Parents or, as the case may be, legal guardians, have the primary responsibility for the upbringing and development of the child. The best interests of the child will be their basic concern.
2. For the purpose of guaranteeing and promoting the rights set forth in the present Convention, States Parties shall render appropriate assistance to parents and legal guardians in the performance of their child-rearing responsibilities and shall ensure the development of institutions, facilities and services for the care of children.
3. States Parties shall take all appropriate measures to ensure that children of working parents have the right to benefit from child-care services and facilities for which they are eligible.

Article 19

1. States Parties shall take all appropriate legislative, administrative, social and educational measures to protect the child from all forms of physical or mental violence, injury or abuse, neglect or negligent treatment, maltreatment or exploitation, including sexual abuse, while in the care of parent(s), legal guardian(s) or any other person who has the care of the child.

2. Such protective measures should, as appropriate, include effective procedures for the establishment of social programmes to provide necessary support for the child and for those who have the care of the child, as well as for other forms of prevention and for identification, reporting, referral, investigation, treatment and follow-up of instances of child maltreatment described heretofore, and, as appropriate, for judicial involvement.

Article 20

1. A child temporarily or permanently deprived of his or her family environment, or in whose own best interests cannot be allowed to remain in that environment, shall be entitled to special protection and assistance provided by the State.
2. States Parties shall in accordance with their national laws ensure alternative care for such a child.
3. Such care could include, inter alia, foster placement, kafalah of Islamic law, adoption or if necessary placement in suitable institutions for the care of children. When considering solutions, due regard shall be paid to the desirability of continuity in a child's upbringing and to the child's ethnic, religious, cultural and linguistic background.

Article 21

States Parties that recognize and/or permit the system of adoption shall ensure that the best interests of the child shall be the paramount consideration and they shall:

(a) Ensure that the adoption of a child is authorized only by competent authorities who determine, in accordance with applicable law and procedures and on the basis of all pertinent and reliable information, that the adoption is permissible in view of the child's status concerning parents, relatives and legal guardians and that, if required, the persons concerned have given their informed consent to the adoption on the basis of such counselling as may be necessary;
(b) Recognize that inter-country adoption may be considered as an alternative means of child's care, if the child cannot be placed in a foster or an adoptive family or cannot in any suitable manner be cared for in the child's country of origin;

(c) Ensure that the child concerned by inter-country adoption enjoys safeguards and standards equivalent to those existing in the case of national adoption;

(d) Take all appropriate measures to ensure that, in inter-country adoption, the placement does not result in improper financial gain for those involved in it;

(e) Promote, where appropriate, the objectives of the present article by concluding bilateral or multilateral arrangements or agreements, and endeavour, within this framework, to ensure that the placement of the child in another country is carried out by competent authorities or organs.

Article 22

1. States Parties shall take appropriate measures to ensure that a child who is seeking refugee status or who is considered a refugee in accordance with applicable international or domestic law and procedures shall, whether unaccompanied or accompanied by his or her parents or by any other person, receive appropriate protection and humanitarian assistance in the enjoyment of applicable rights set forth in the present Convention and in other international human rights or humanitarian instruments to which the said States are Parties.

2. For this purpose, States Parties shall provide, as they consider appropriate, co-operation in any efforts by the United Nations and other competent intergovernmental organizations or non-governmental organizations co-operating with the United Nations to protect and assist such a child and to trace the parents or other members of the family of any refugee child in order to obtain information necessary for reunification with his or her family. In cases where no parents or other members of the family can be found, the child shall be accorded the same protection as any other child permanently or temporarily deprived of his or her family environment for any reason, as set forth in the present Convention.

Article 23

1. States Parties recognize that a mentally or physically disabled child should enjoy a full and decent life, in conditions which ensure dignity, promote self-reliance and facilitate the child's active participation in the community.

2. States Parties recognize the right of the disabled child to special care and shall encourage and ensure the extension, subject to available resources, to the eligible child and those responsible for his or her care, of assistance for which application is made and which is appropriate to the child's condition and to the circumstances of the parents or others caring for the child.

3. Recognizing the special needs of a disabled child, assistance extended in accordance with paragraph 2 of the present article shall be provided free of charge, whenever possible, taking into account the financial resources of the parents or others caring for the child, and shall be designed to ensure that the disabled child has effective access to and receives education, training, health care services, rehabilitation services, preparation for employment and recreation opportunities in a manner conducive to the child's achieving the fullest possible social integration and individual development, including his or her cultural and spiritual development

4. States Parties shall promote, in the spirit of international cooperation, the exchange of appropriate information in the field of preventive health care and of medical, psychological and functional treatment of disabled children, including dissemination of and access to information concerning methods of rehabilitation, education and vocational services, with the aim of enabling States Parties to improve their capabilities and skills and to widen their experience in these areas. In this regard, particular account shall be taken of the needs of developing countries.

Article 24

1. States Parties recognize the right of the child to the enjoyment of the highest attainable standard of health and to facilities for the treatment of illness and rehabilitation of health. States Parties shall strive to ensure that no child is deprived of his or her right of access to such health care services.

2. States Parties shall pursue full implementation of this right and, in particular, shall take appropriate measures:
   (a) To diminish infant and child mortality;
   (b) To ensure the provision of necessary medical assistance and health care to all children with emphasis on the development of primary health care;
   (c) To combat disease and malnutrition, including within the framework of primary health care, through, inter alia, the

application of readily available technology and through the provision of adequate nutritious foods and clean drinking-water, taking into consideration the dangers and risks of environmental pollution;

(d) To ensure appropriate pre-natal and post-natal health care for mothers;

(e) To ensure that all segments of society, in particular parents and children, are informed, have access to education and are supported in the use of basic knowledge of child health and nutrition, the advantages of breastfeeding, hygiene and environmental sanitation and the prevention of accidents;

(f) To develop preventive health care, guidance for parents and family planning education and services.

3. States Parties shall take all effective and appropriate measures with a view to abolishing traditional practices prejudicial to the health of children.

4. States Parties undertake to promote and encourage international co-operation with a view to achieving progressively the full realization of the right recognized in the present article. In this regard, particular account shall be taken of the needs of developing countries.

Article 25

States Parties recognize the right of a child who has been placed by the competent authorities for the purposes of care, protection or treatment of his or her physical or mental health, to a periodic review of the treatment provided to the child and all other circumstances relevant to his or her placement.

Article 26

1. States Parties shall recognize for every child the right to benefit from social security, including social insurance, and shall take the necessary measures to achieve the full realization of this right in accordance with their national law.

2. The benefits should, where appropriate, be granted, taking into account the resources and the circumstances of the child and persons having responsibility for the maintenance of the child, as well as any other consideration relevant to an application for benefits made by or on behalf of the child.

Article 27

1. States Parties recognize the right of every child to a standard of living adequate for the child's physical, mental, spiritual, moral and social development.
2. The parent(s) or others responsible for the child have the primary responsibility to secure, within their abilities and financial capacities, the conditions of living necessary for the child's development.
3. States Parties, in accordance with national conditions and within their means, shall take appropriate measures to assist parents and others responsible for the child to implement this right and shall in case of need provide material assistance and support programmes, particularly with regard to nutrition, clothing and housing.
4. States Parties shall take all appropriate measures to secure the recovery of maintenance for the child from the parents or other persons having financial responsibility for the child, both within the State Party and from abroad. In particular, where the person having financial responsibility for the child lives in a State different from that of the child, States Parties shall promote the accession to international agreements or the conclusion of such agreements, as well as the making of other appropriate arrangements.

Article 28

1. States Parties recognize the right of the child to education, and with a view to achieving this right progressively and on the basis of equal opportunity, they shall, in particular:
   (a) Make primary education compulsory and available free to all;
   (b) Encourage the development of different forms of secondary education, including general and vocational education, make them available and accessible to every child, and take appropriate measures such as the introduction of free education and offering financial assistance in case of need;
   (c) Make higher education accessible to all on the basis of capacity by every appropriate means;
   (d) Make educational and vocational information and guidance available and accessible to all children;
   (e) Take measures to encourage regular attendance at schools and the reduction of drop-out rates.
2. States Parties shall take all appropriate measures to ensure that school discipline is administered in a manner consistent with the

child's human dignity and in conformity with the present Convention.

3. States Parties shall promote and encourage international cooper-
    ation in matters relating to education, in particular with a view
    to contributing to the elimination of ignorance and illiteracy
    throughout the world and facilitating access to scientific and tech-
    nical knowledge and modern teaching methods. In this regard,
    particular account shall be taken of the needs of developing coun-
    tries.

Article 29

1. States Parties agree that the education of the child shall be directed
    to:
    (a) The development of the child's personality, talents and men-
         tal and physical abilities to their fullest potential;
    (b) The development of respect for human rights and fundamen-
         tal freedoms, and for the principles enshrined in the Charter
         of the United Nations;
    (c) The development of respect for the child's parents, his or her
         own cultural identity, language and values, for the national
         values of the country in which the child is living, the coun-
         try from which he or she may originate, and for civilizations
         different from his or her own;
    (d) The preparation of the child for responsible life in a free soci-
         ety, in the spirit of understanding, peace, tolerance, equality
         of sexes, and friendship among all peoples, ethnic, national
         and religious groups and persons of indigenous origin;
    (e) The development of respect for the natural environment.
2. No part of the present article or article 28 shall be construed so
    as to interfere with the liberty of individuals and bodies to es-
    tablish and direct educational institutions, subject always to the
    observance of the principle set forth in paragraph 1 of the present
    article and to the requirements that the education given in such
    institutions shall conform to such minimum standards as may be
    laid down by the State.

Article 30

In those States in which ethnic, religious or linguistic minorities or persons
of indigenous origin exist, a child belonging to such a minority or who
is indigenous shall not be denied the right, in community with other

members of his or her group, to enjoy his or her own culture, to profess and practise his or her own religion, or to use his or her own language.

Article 31

1. States Parties recognize the right of the child to rest and leisure, to engage in play and recreational activities appropriate to the age of the child and to participate freely in cultural life and the arts.
2. States Parties shall respect and promote the right of the child to participate fully in cultural and artistic life and shall encourage the provision of appropriate and equal opportunities for cultural, artistic, recreational and leisure activity.

Article 32

1. States Parties recognize the right of the child to be protected from economic exploitation and from performing any work that is likely to be hazardous or to interfere with the child's education, or to be harmful to the child's health or physical, mental, spiritual, moral or social development.
2. States Parties shall take legislative, administrative, social and educational measures to ensure the implementation of the present article. To this end, and having regard to the relevant provisions of other international instruments, States Parties shall in particular:
   (a) Provide for a minimum age or minimum ages for admission to employment;
   (b) Provide for appropriate regulation of the hours and conditions of employment;
   (c) Provide for appropriate penalties or other sanctions to ensure the effective enforcement of the present article.

Article 33

States Parties shall take all appropriate measures, including legislative, administrative, social and educational measures, to protect children from the illicit use of narcotic drugs and psychotropic substances as defined in the relevant international treaties, and to prevent the use of children in the illicit production and trafficking of such substances.

Article 34

States Parties undertake to protect the child from all forms of sexual exploitation and sexual abuse. For these purposes, States Parties shall in particular take all appropriate national, bilateral and multilateral measures to prevent:

(a) The inducement or coercion of a child to engage in any unlawful sexual activity;
(b) The exploitative use of children in prostitution or other unlawful sexual practices;
(c) The exploitative use of children in pornographic performances and materials.

Article 35

States Parties shall take all appropriate national, bilateral and multilateral measures to prevent the abduction of, the sale of or traffic in children for any purpose or in any form.

Article 36

States Parties shall protect the child against all other forms of exploitation prejudicial to any aspects of the child's welfare.

Article 37

States Parties shall ensure that:

(a) No child shall be subjected to torture or other cruel, inhuman or degrading treatment or punishment. Neither capital punishment nor life imprisonment without possibility of release shall be imposed for offences committed by persons below eighteen years of age;
(b) No child shall be deprived of his or her liberty unlawfully or arbitrarily. The arrest, detention or imprisonment of a child shall be in conformity with the law and shall be used only as a measure of last resort and for the shortest appropriate period of time;

(c) Every child deprived of liberty shall be treated with humanity and respect for the inherent dignity of the human person, and in a manner which takes into account the needs of persons of his or her age. In particular, every child deprived of liberty shall be separated from adults unless it is considered in the child's best interest not to do so and shall have the right to maintain contact with his or her family through correspondence and visits, save in exceptional circumstances;

(d) Every child deprived of his or her liberty shall have the right to prompt access to legal and other appropriate assistance, as well as the right to challenge the legality of the deprivation of his or her liberty before a court or other competent, independent and impartial authority, and to a prompt decision on any such action.

Article 38

1. States Parties undertake to respect and to ensure respect for rules of international humanitarian law applicable to them in armed conflicts which are relevant to the child.
2. States Parties shall take all feasible measures to ensure that persons who have not attained the age of fifteen years do not take a direct part in hostilities.
3. States Parties shall refrain from recruiting any person who has not attained the age of fifteen years into their armed forces. In recruiting among those persons who have attained the age of fifteen years but who have not attained the age of eighteen years, States Parties shall endeavour to give priority to those who are oldest.
4. In accordance with their obligations under international humanitarian law to protect the civilian population in armed conflicts, States Parties shall take all feasible measures to ensure protection and care of children who are affected by an armed conflict.

Article 39

States Parties shall take all appropriate measures to promote physical and psychological recovery and social reintegration of a child victim of: any form of neglect, exploitation, or abuse; torture or any other form of cruel, inhuman or degrading treatment or punishment; or armed conflicts. Such recovery and reintegration shall take place in an environment which fosters the health, self-respect and dignity of the child.

Article 40

1. States Parties recognize the right of every child alleged as, accused of, or recognized as having infringed the penal law to be treated in a manner consistent with the promotion of the child's sense of dignity and worth, which reinforces the child's respect for the human rights and fundamental freedoms of others and which takes into account the child's age and the desirability of promoting the child's reintegration and the child's assuming a constructive role in society.
2. To this end, and having regard to the relevant provisions of international instruments, States Parties shall, in particular, ensure that:
   (a) No child shall be alleged as, be accused of, or recognized as having infringed the penal law by reason of acts or omissions that were not prohibited by national or international law at the time they were committed;
   (b) Every child alleged as or accused of having infringed the penal law has at least the following guarantees:
   (i) To be presumed innocent until proven guilty according to law;
   (ii) To be informed promptly and directly of the charges against him or her, and, if appropriate, through his or her parents or legal guardians, and to have legal or other appropriate assistance in the preparation and presentation of his or her defence;
   (iii) To have the matter determined without delay by a competent, independent and impartial authority or judicial body in a fair hearing according to law, in the presence of legal or other appropriate assistance and, unless it is considered not to be in the best interest of the child, in particular, taking into account his or her age or situation, his or her parents or legal guardians;
   (iv) Not to be compelled to give testimony or to confess guilt; to examine or have examined adverse witnesses and to obtain the participation and examination of witnesses on his or her behalf under conditions of equality;
   (v) If considered to have infringed the penal law, to have this decision and any measures imposed in consequence thereof reviewed by a higher competent, independent and impartial authority or judicial body according to law;

      (vi) To have the free assistance of an interpreter if the child cannot understand or speak the language used;

     (vii) To have his or her privacy fully respected at all stages of the proceedings.

3. States Parties shall seek to promote the establishment of laws, procedures, authorities and institutions specifically applicable to children alleged as, accused of, or recognized as having infringed the penal law, and, in particular:

    (a) The establishment of a minimum age below which children shall be presumed not to have the capacity to infringe the penal law;

    (b) Whenever appropriate and desirable, measures for dealing with such children without resorting to judicial proceedings, providing that human rights and legal safeguards are fully respected.

4. A variety of dispositions, such as care, guidance and supervision orders; counselling; probation; foster care; education and vocational training programmes and other alternatives to institutional care shall be available to ensure that children are dealt with in a manner appropriate to their well-being and proportionate both to their circumstances and the offence.

Article 41

Nothing in the present Convention shall affect any provisions which are more conducive to the realization of the rights of the child and which may be contained in:

(a) The law of a State party; or

(b) International law in force for that State.

PART II

Article 42

States Parties undertake to make the principles and provisions of the Convention widely known, by appropriate and active means, to adults and children alike.

Article 43

1. For the purpose of examining the progress made by States Parties in achieving the realization of the obligations undertaken in the present Convention, there shall be established a Committee on the Rights of the Child, which shall carry out the functions hereinafter provided.
2. The Committee shall consist of eighteen experts of high moral standing and recognized competence in the field covered by this Convention.[1] The members of the Committee shall be elected by States Parties from among their nationals and shall serve in their personal capacity, consideration being given to equitable geographical distribution, as well as to the principal legal systems.
3. The members of the Committee shall be elected by secret ballot from a list of persons nominated by States Parties. Each State Party may nominate one person from among its own nationals.
4. The initial election to the Committee shall be held no later than six months after the date of the entry into force of the present Convention and thereafter every second year. At least four months before the date of each election, the Secretary-General of the United Nations shall address a letter to States Parties inviting them to submit their nominations within two months. The Secretary-General shall subsequently prepare a list in alphabetical order of all persons thus nominated, indicating States Parties which have nominated them, and shall submit it to the States Parties to the present Convention.
5. The elections shall be held at meetings of States Parties convened by the Secretary-General at United Nations Headquarters. At those meetings, for which two thirds of States Parties shall constitute a quorum, the persons elected to the Committee shall be those who obtain the largest number of votes and an absolute majority of the votes of the representatives of States Parties present and voting.
6. The members of the Committee shall be elected for a term of four years. They shall be eligible for re-election if renominated. The term of five of the members elected at the first election shall

---

[1] The General Assembly, in its resolution 50/155 of 21 December 1995, approved the amendment to article 43, paragraph 2, of the Convention on the Rights of the Child, replacing the word "ten" with the word "eighteen". The amendment entered into force on 18 November 2002 when it had been accepted by a two-thirds majority of the States parties (128 out of 191).

expire at the end of two years; immediately after the first election, the names of these five members shall be chosen by lot by the Chairman of the meeting.

7. If a member of the Committee dies or resigns or declares that for any other cause he or she can no longer perform the duties of the Committee, the State Party which nominated the member shall appoint another expert from among its nationals to serve for the remainder of the term, subject to the approval of the Committee.

8. The Committee shall establish its own rules of procedure.

9. The Committee shall elect its officers for a period of two years.

10. The meetings of the Committee shall normally be held at United Nations Headquarters or at any other convenient place as determined by the Committee. The Committee shall normally meet annually. The duration of the meetings of the Committee shall be determined, and reviewed, if necessary, by a meeting of the States Parties to the present Convention, subject to the approval of the General Assembly.

11. The Secretary-General of the United Nations shall provide the necessary staff and facilities for the effective performance of the functions of the Committee under the present Convention.

12. With the approval of the General Assembly, the members of the Committee established under the present Convention shall receive emoluments from United Nations resources on such terms and conditions as the Assembly may decide.

Article 44

1. States Parties undertake to submit to the Committee, through the Secretary-General of the United Nations, reports on the measures they have adopted which give effect to the rights recognized herein and on the progress made on the enjoyment of those rights
   (a) Within two years of the entry into force of the Convention for the State Party concerned;
   (b) Thereafter every five years.

2. Reports made under the present article shall indicate factors and difficulties, if any, affecting the degree of fulfilment of the obligations under the present Convention. Reports shall also contain sufficient information to provide the Committee with a comprehensive understanding of the implementation of the Convention in the country concerned.

3. A State Party which has submitted a comprehensive initial report to the Committee need not, in its subsequent reports submitted

in accordance with paragraph 1 (b) of the present article, repeat basic information previously provided.

4. The Committee may request from States Parties further information relevant to the implementation of the Convention.
5. The Committee shall submit to the General Assembly, through the Economic and Social Council, every two years, reports on its activities.
6. States Parties shall make their reports widely available to the public in their own countries.

Article 45

In order to foster the effective implementation of the Convention and to encourage international co-operation in the field covered by the Convention:

(a) The specialized agencies, the United Nations Children's Fund, and other United Nations organs shall be entitled to be represented at the consideration of the implementation of such provisions of the present Convention as fall within the scope of their mandate. The Committee may invite the specialized agencies, the United Nations Children's Fund and other competent bodies as it may consider appropriate to provide expert advice on the implementation of the Convention in areas falling within the scope of their respective mandates. The Committee may invite the specialized agencies, the United Nations Children's Fund, and other United Nations organs to submit reports on the implementation of the Convention in areas falling within the scope of their activities;

(b) The Committee shall transmit, as it may consider appropriate, to the specialized agencies, the United Nations Children's Fund and other competent bodies, any reports from States Parties that contain a request, or indicate a need, for technical advice or assistance, along with the Committee's observations and suggestions, if any, on these requests or indications;

(c) The Committee may recommend to the General Assembly to request the Secretary-General to undertake on its behalf studies on specific issues relating to the rights of the child;

(d) The Committee may make suggestions and general recommendations based on information received pursuant to articles 44 and 45 of the present Convention. Such suggestions and general recommendations shall be transmitted to any State Party concerned and reported to the General Assembly, together with comments, if any, from States Parties.

PART III

Article 46

The present Convention shall be open for signature by all States.

Article 47

The present Convention is subject to ratification. Instruments of ratification shall be deposited with the Secretary-General of the United Nations.

Article 48

The present Convention shall remain open for accession by any State. The instruments of accession shall be deposited with the Secretary-General of the United Nations.

Article 49

1. The present Convention shall enter into force on the thirtieth day following the date of deposit with the Secretary-General of the United Nations of the twentieth instrument of ratification or accession.
2. For each State ratifying or acceding to the Convention after the deposit of the twentieth instrument of ratification or accession, the Convention shall enter into force on the thirtieth day after the deposit by such State of its instrument of ratification or accession.

Article 50

1. Any State Party may propose an amendment and file it with the Secretary-General of the United Nations. The Secretary-General shall thereupon communicate the proposed amendment to States Parties, with a request that they indicate whether they favour a

conference of States Parties for the purpose of considering and voting upon the proposals. In the event that, within four months from the date of such communication, at least one third of the States Parties favour such a conference, the Secretary-General shall convene the conference under the auspices of the United Nations. Any amendment adopted by a majority of States Parties present and voting at the conference shall be submitted to the General Assembly for approval.

2. An amendment adopted in accordance with paragraph 1 of the present article shall enter into force when it has been approved by the General Assembly of the United Nations and accepted by a two-thirds majority of States Parties.

3. When an amendment enters into force, it shall be binding on those States Parties which have accepted it, other States Parties still being bound by the provisions of the present Convention and any earlier amendments which they have accepted.

Article 51

1. The Secretary-General of the United Nations shall receive and circulate to all States the text of reservations made by States at the time of ratification or accession.

2. A reservation incompatible with the object and purpose of the present Convention shall not be permitted.

3. Reservations may be withdrawn at any time by notification to that effect addressed to the Secretary-General of the United Nations, who shall then inform all States. Such notification shall take effect on the date on which it is received by the Secretary-General.

Article 52

A State Party may denounce the present Convention by written notification to the Secretary-General of the United Nations. Denunciation becomes effective one year after the date of receipt of the notification by the Secretary-General.

Article 53

The Secretary-General of the United Nations is designated as the depositary of the present Convention.

Article 54

The original of the present Convention, of which the Arabic, Chinese, English, French, Russian and Spanish texts are equally authentic, shall be deposited with the Secretary-General of the United Nations. In witness thereof the undersigned plenipotentiaries, being duly authorized thereto by their respective Governments, have signed the present Convention.

References

Alderson, P. (2000a) School students' views on school councils and daily life at school, *Children and Society,* 14(2) 121–34.

Alderson, P. (2000b) Practising democracy in two inner city schools, in A. Osler (ed) *Citizenship and Democracy in Schools: Diversity, Identity, Equality.* Stoke-on-Trent: Trentham.

Alderson, P. and Goodwin, M. (1993) Contradictions within concepts of children's competence, *International Journal of Children's Rights,* 1: 303–13.

Ameli, S.R., Marandi, S.M., Ahmed, S., Kara, S. and Merali, A. (2007) *The British Media and Muslim Representation: The Ideology of Demonisation.* Wembley: Islamic Human Rights Commission.

Apple, M.W. (1993) *Official Knowledge: Democratic Education in a Conservative Age.* New York/London: Routledge.

Apple, M.W. and Beane, J.A. (1999) *Democratic Schools: Lessons from the Chalkface.* Buckingham: Open University Press.

Arnot, M. and Raey, D. (2004) The social dynamics of classroom learning, in M. Arnot, D. McIntyre, D. Pedder and D. Raey (eds) *Consultation in the Classroom.* Cambridge: Pearson.

Banks, J.A., McGee Banks, C.A., Cotes, C.E., et al. (2005) *Democracy and Diversity: Principles and Concepts for Educating Citizens In a Global Age.* Seattle: University of Washington, Center for Multicultural Education, available online at www.education.washington.edu/cme/DemDiv.pdf (accessed 27 October 2009).

Berkeley, R. (2008) *Right to Divide? Faith Schools and Community Cohesion.* London: Runnymede Trust.

Blair, M. (2001) *Why Pick on Me? Exclusion and Black Youth.* Trentham: Stoke-on-Trent.

Blair, T. (2006) Our nation's future: multiculturalism and integration. Speech given at 10 Downing Street, 8 December, available online at www.number10.gov.uk/output/Page10563.asp (accessed 3 August 2007).

British Educational Research Association (BERA) (2004) *Revised Ethical Guidelines for Educational Research (2004)*; available online at www.bera.ac.uk/ (accessed 21 August 2009).

British Educational Research Association (BERA) (2009) *Research Methodology in Education Special Interest Group,* available online at www.bera.ac. uk/methodology/ (accessed 27 October 2009).

Brown, G. (2006) Who do we want to be? The future of Britishness. Speech given to the Fabian Society, 16 January, available online at fabians. org.uk/events/new-year-conference-06/brown-britishness/speech (accessed 3 August 2007).

Carter, C. and Osler, A. (2000) Human rights, identities and conflict management: a study of school culture as experienced through classroom relationships, *Cambridge Journal of Education,* 30(3): 335–56.

Christensen, P. Haudrup (2004) Children's participation in ethnographic research: issues of power and representation, *Children and Society,* 18: 165–76.

Commission for Racial Equality (CRE) (2007) *A Lot Done, a Lot to Do: Our Vision for an Integrated Britain.* London: CRE.

Commission on Integration and Cohesion (COIC) (2007) *Interim Statement from the Commission on Integration and Cohesion.* Department for Communities and Local Government, London, available online at www.integrationand_cohesion.org.uk

Commission on the Future of Multi-Ethnic Britain (CFMEB) (2000) *The Future of Multi-ethnic Britain. The Parekh Report.* London: Profile Books.

Committee on the Rights of the Child (2002) *Concluding Observations of the Committee on the Rights of the Child: United Kingdom of Great Britain and Northern Ireland. UN/CRC/C/15/Add.188.* Geneva: United Nations.

Committee on the Rights of the Child (2008) *Concluding Observations of the Committee on the Rights of the Child: United Kingdom of Great Britain and Northern Ireland.* CRC/C/GBR/CO/4, 3 October, available online at www.crin.org/resources/infoDetail.asp?ID=18572&flag=legal (accessed from Child Rights Information Network, 15 July 2009).

Council of Europe (1985) *Recommendation R (85) 7 of the Committee of Ministers of Member States on Teaching and Learning about Human Rights in Schools.* Adopted by the Committee of Ministers on 14 May at the 385th meeting of the Ministers' Deputies. Strasbourg: Council of Europe.

David, M., Edwards, R. and Alldred, P. (2001) Children and school-based research: 'informed consent' or 'educated consent'? *British Educational Research Journal,* 27(1): 347–65.

Davies, L. and Kirkpatrick, G. (2000) *The Euridem Project: A Review of Pupil Democracy in Europe.* London: Children's Rights Alliance for England.

Department for Children, Schools and Families (DCSF) (undated) *Every Child Matters,* available online at www.dcsf.gov.uk/everychildmatters/ (accessed 4 September 2009).

Department for Children, Schools and Families (DCSF) (undated) *Extended Schools*, available online at www.standards.dfes.gov.uk/studysupport/ impact/extendedschools/ (accessed 5 September 2009).

Department for Children, Schools and Families (DCSF) (2007) *Guidance on the Duty to Promote Community Cohesion*. London: DCSF, available online at www.publications.teachernet.gov.uk/default.aspx? PageFunction=productdetails&PageMode=publications&ProductId= DCSF-00598-2007& (accessed 28 October 2009).

Dewey, J. ([1916] 2002) Democracy and education: an introduction to the philosophy of education, in S.J. Maxcy (ed.) *John Dewey and American Education*, Vol. 3. Bristol: Thoemmes.

Dewey, J. (1940) Creative democracy: the task before us, in S. Ratner (ed.) *The Philosophy of the Common Man: Essays in Honor of John Dewey to Celebrate his 80th Birthday* (pp. 220–8). New York: Putnam.

Eekelaar, J. (1986) The emergence of children's rights, *Oxford Journal of Legal Studies*, 6: 161–82.

Etzioni, A. (1995) *The Spirit of Community*. London: Fontana.

English Secondary Students Association (ESSA) (2009) Available online at www.studentvoice.co.uk/index.html (accessed 21 August 2009).

Family Law Week (2005) Mabon v Mabon and Others [2005] EWCA Civ 634 Independent representation of articulate teenagers under FPR 1991, rule 9.2A allowed on appeal. Court of Appeal: Thorpe, Latham and Wall LJJ (26 May 2005), available online at www.familylawweek. co.uk/site.aspx?i=ed203 (accessed 14 July 2009).

Feinberg, J. (1980) The child's right to an open future, in W. Aiken and H. LaFollettee (eds) *Whose Child?* Totowa, NJ: Littlefield Adams.

Fielding, M. (2004) 'New wave' student voice and the renewal of civic society, *London Review of Education*, 2(3): 197–217.

Figueroa, P. (2004) Multicultural education in the United Kingdom: historical development and current status, in J.A. Banks and C.A. McGee Banks (eds) *Handbook of Research on Multicultural Education*, 2nd edn (pp. 219–44). San Francisco, CA: Jossey Bass.

Freeman, M. (1988) Taking children's rights seriously, *Children and Society*, 4: 299–319.

Freeman, M. (1996) Children's education: a test case for best interests and autonomy, in R. Davie and D. Galloway (eds) *Listening to Children in Education*. London: David Fulton.

Freeman, M. (2000) The future of children's rights, *Children and Society*, 14: 277–93.

Gillick v. Wisbech and West Norfolk AHA. [1985] 3 All ER.

Grover, S. (2007) Children's right to be educated for tolerance: minority rights and inclusion, *Education and the Law*, 19(1): 59–70.

Hahn, C.L. (1999) Citizenship education: an empirical study of policies, practices and outcomes, *Oxford Review of Education*, 25(1/2):231–50.

Hallett, C and Prout, A. (2003) (eds) *Hearing the Voices of Children: Social Policy for a New Century*. London: RoutledgeFalmer.

Hansard (1972) *Deb 15 June 1972 vol 838 cc1697-8 15 June. Education and Science*, available online at www. hansard.millbanksystems. com/commons/1972/jun/15/national-union-of-school-students

Harber, C. (2002) Education, democracy and poverty reduction in Africa, *Comparative Education*, 38(3): 267–76.

Harber, C. (2004) *Schooling as Violence: How Schools Harm Pupils and Societies*. London: RoutledgeFalmer.

Harber, C. (2008) Perpetrating disaffection: schooling as an international problem, *Educational Studies*, 34(5): 457–67.

Hill, M., Graham, C., Caulfield, C., Ross, N. and Shelton, A. (2007) Interethnic relations among children at school: the perspectives of young people in Scotland, *European Journal of Education*, 42(2): 267–79.

Home Office (2001) *Community Cohesion: A Report of the Independent Review Team. The Cantle Report*. Home Office, London, available online at: www.image.guardian.co.uk/sys-files/Guardian/documents/ 2001/12/11/communitycohesionreport.pdf (accessed 7 September 2007).

House of Commons Children, Schools and Families Committee (2009) *Diversity of School Provision*. Oral and written evidence to the Children, Schools and Families Committee. HC 432 (incorporating HC 311-i to -v Session 2007–08) 5 May. London: The Stationery Office, available online at www.publications.parliament.uk/pa/cm200809/ cmselect/cmchilsch/432/432.pdf (accessed 1 September 2009).

Hudson, A. (2005) Citizenship education and students' identities: a school-based action research project, in A. Osler (ed.) *Teachers, Human Rights and Diversity: Educating Citizens in a Multicultural Society*. Stoke-on-Trent: Trentham.

Hughes, L. ([1938] 1994) Let America be America again, in A. Rampersad and Roessel (eds) *The Collected Poems of Langston Hughes*. New York: Vintage.

Jawad, H. and Benn, T. (eds) (2003) *Muslim Women in the United Kingdom and Beyond: Experiences and Images*. Leiden: Brill.

Kenway, J. (2003) Foreword, in A. Osler and K. Vincent (eds) *Girls and Exclusion: Rethinking the Agenda*. London: Routledge.

Kilbourne, S. (1998) The wayward Americans: why the USA has not ratified the UN Convention on the Rights of the Child, *Child and Family Law Quarterly* 10(3): 1–15.

Kilkenny, U., Kilpatrick, R., Lundy, L., et al. (2004) *Children's Rights in Northern Ireland*. Belfast: Northern Ireland Commissioner for

Children and Young People, available online at www.niccy.org/article. aspx?menuId=381 (accessed 9 September 2009).

Kirby, P., Hays Young researchers, Wubner, K. and Lewis M. (2001) The Hays project: young people in control? In J. Clark, A. Dyson, N. Meagher, E. Robson and M. Wootten (eds) *Young People as Researchers: Possibilities, Problems and Politics*. Leicester: Youth Work Press.

Lansdown, G. (1995) *Taking Part: Children's Participation in Decision-making*. London: Institute for Public Policy Research.

Lansdown, G. (2001) *Promoting Children's Participation in Democratic Decision-making*. Florence: UNICEF Innocenti Research Centre, available online at www.unicef-irc.org/cgi-bin/unicef/download_insert. sql?ProductID=290 (accessed 23 August 2009).

Lansdown, G. and Newell, P. (1994) *UK Agenda for Children*. London: Children's Rights Development Unit.

Los Angeles Times (2009) 4 September, available online at www.latimes. com/news/nationworld/nation/la-na-obama-schoolkids4-2009sep04, 01237265.story (accessed 5 September 2009).

Lundy, L. (2007) 'Voice' is not enough: conceptualizing Article 132 of the United Nations Convention on the Rights of the Child, *British Educational Research Journal,* 33(6): 927–42.

MacAskill, E. (2009) Obama tones down his appeal to pupils after indoctrination claims, *The Guardian*, 5 September: 19.

Magadi, M. and Middleton, S (2005) *Britain's Poorest Children Revisited: Evidence from BHPS (1994–2002)*, CRSP Research Report 3, Loughborough University.

Magadi, M. and Middleton, S. (2007) *Severe Child Poverty in the UK*. London: Save the Children.

Mayall, B. (2000) Conversations with children: working with generational issues, in P.M. Christensen and A. James (eds) *Research with Children: Perspectives and Practices*. London: Falmer.

Meighan, R. (1978) A pupil's eye view of teaching performance, *Educational Review,* 30(2): 125–37.

Mitchell, K. and Parker, W.C. (2008) I pledge allegiance to . . . flexible citizenship an shifting scales of belonging, *Teachers College Record,* 110, 4: 775–804.

Morrow, V. (1999) 'We are people too': children's and young people's perspectives on children's rights and decision-making in England, *International Journal of Children's Rights,* 7: 149–70.

Morrow, V. (2001) Using qualitative methods to elicit young people's perspectives on their environments: some ideas for community health initiatives, *Health Education Research,* 16(3): 255–68.

National Children's Bureau (NCB) (2003) *Guidelines for Research*. London: National Children's Bureau, available online at www.ncb.org.uk/

about_us/our_structure/research_policy_participation/research.aspx (accessed 20 August 2009).

Obama, B. (2008) Walden University Presidential Youth Debate, October, available online at www.debate.waldenu.edu/video/question-12/ #content (accessed 13 July 2009).

Osler, A. (1997) *The Education and Careers of Black Teachers: Changing Identities, Changing Lives.* Buckingham: Open University Press.

Osler, A. (2006) Multicultural schools and classrooms: using the voices of children and young people to inform policy and practice, in C. Baraldi (ed.) *Education and Intercultural Narratives in Multicultural Classrooms.* Rome: Officina Edizioni.

Osler, A. (2007) *Faith Schools and Community Cohesion.* London: Runnymede Trust.

Osler, A. (2009a) Testing citizenship and allegiance: policy, politics and the education of adult migrants in the UK, *Education, Citizenship and Social Justice,* 4(1): 63–79.

Osler, A. (2009b) Patriotism, multiculturalism and belonging: political discourse and the teaching of history, *Educational Review,* 61(1):85–100.

Osler, A. (2009c) Citizenship education, democracy and racial justice 10 years on, *Race Equality Teaching,* 27(3): 21–7.

Osler, A. (forthcoming) Teacher interpretations of citizenship education: national identity, cosmopolitan ideals, and political realities, *Journal of Curriculum Studies.*

Osler, A. and Hill, J. (1999) Exclusion from school and racial equality: an examination of government proposals in the light of recent research evidence, *Cambridge Journal of Education,* 29(1): 38–62.

Osler, A. and Osler, C. (2002) Inclusion, exclusion and children's rights: a case study of a student with Asperger Syndrome, *Journal of Emotional and Behavioural Difficulties,* 7(1): 35–54.

Osler, A. and Starkey, H. (2003) Learning for cosmopolitan citizenship: theoretical debates and young people's experiences, *Educational Review,* 55(3): 243–54.

Osler, A. and Starkey, H. (2005) *Changing Citizenship: Democracy and Inclusion in Education.* Buckingham: Open University Press.

Osler A. and Vincent, K. (2002) *Citizenship and the Challenge of Global Education.* Stoke-on-Trent: Trentham.

Osler, A. and Vincent, K. (2003) *Girls and Exclusion: Rethinking the Agenda.* London: RoutledgeFalmer.

Parker, W.C. (2008) 'International Education' – what's in a name? *Phi Delta Kappan,* 90(2): 196–202.

Parker, W.C. and Camicia, S.P. (2009) Cognitive praxis in today's 'international education' movement: a case study of intents and affinities,

Theory and Research in Social Education, 37(1): 42–74, available online at www.un.org/millenniumgoals/education.shtml (accessed 6 April 2009).

Phillips, T. (2005) After 7/7: Sleepwalking to segregation. Speech to the Manchester Council for Community Relations, 22 September, available online at www.cre.gov.uk/Default.aspx.LocID-0hgnew07s. RefLocID-0hg00900c002.Lang-EN.htm#top (accessed 24 August 2007).

Pollard A. and Filer, A. (1996) *The Social World of Children's Learning: Case Studies of Pupil from Four to Seven*. London: Cassell.

Ranson, S. (2000) Recognizing the pedagogy of voice in a learning community, *Educational Management Administration and Leadership*, 28(3): 263–79.

Richardson, R. (1997) *Islamophobia: A Challenge for Us All*. London: Runnymede Trust.

Rodham, H. (1973) Children under the law, *Harvard Educational Review*, 43: 487–514.

Rudduck, J., Chaplain, R. and Wallace, G. (1996) *School Improvement; What Can Pupils Tell US?* London: David Fulton.

Rudduck, J. and Flutter, J. (2004) *How to Improve your School: Giving Pupils a Voice*. London: Continuum.

Rudduck, J. and McIntyre, D. (2007) *Improving Learning through Consulting Pupils*. Abingdon: Routledge.

The Guardian (2009) 7 June, available on line at www.guardian.co.uk/politics/2009/jun/07/european-elections-manchester-liverpool (accessed 8 June 2009).

Tomlinson, S. (2005) Race, ethnicity and education under New Labour, *Oxford Review of Education*, 31(1): 153–71.

United Nations Children's Fund (UNICEF) (2007) *Child Poverty in Perspective: An Overview of Child Well-being in Rich Countries*. Florence: UNICEF Innocenti Research Centre, Innocenti Report Card 7.

US Department of Education (2009) *Menu of Classroom Activities: President Obama's Address to Students Across America (PreK-6)*. Produced by Teaching Ambassador Fellows, available online at www.ed.gov/results.html?q=speech+8+September&cx=017789009494528204701%3Auzmeqn9qqxo&cof=FORID%3A9&hq=-archived%3A&ie=UTF-8&sa.x=19&sa.y=12#1105 (accessed 28 October 2009).

Van Bueren, G. (1995) *The International Law on the Rights of the Child*. Dordrecht: Martinus Nijhoff.

Verhellen, E. (2000) Children's rights and education, in A. Osler (ed.) *Citizenship and Democracy in Schools: Diversity, Identity, Equality*. Stoke-on-Trent: Trentham.

West, A. and Allen, R. (2008) *Diversity of School Provision: Faith Schools, Memorandum Submitted to the House of Commons Select Committee on Children, Schools and Families.* London: HMSO.

White, J. (2004) Should religious education be a compulsory school subject? *British Journal of Religious Education*, 26(2): 151–64.

Woods, P. (1976) Pupil views of school, *Educational Review*, 28: 126–37.

Woods, P. (1978) Relating to schoolwork: some pupil perceptions, *Educational Review*, 30(2): 167–75.

Woods, P. (1980) *Pupil Strategies.* London: Croom Helm.

Index

American Supreme Court 89, 90
Anonymity *see also* ethics *and* research methodologies
   challenges 32, 47
   in research context 32, 46
Apartheid 121–2

Blair, Tony, MP 93, 95
Brown, Gordon, MP 93, 95
Bullying 102, 103, 108
   as a barrier to learning 112
   as a factor in school exclusions 101–2
   impact on victims 87

Child poverty 91, 120
   national levels of 73–4
Child protection 53, 109
   in research context 32, 39
   right to protection 106
Children *see also* young people *and* students
   as a marginalized group 26, 29, 56
   autonomy of 22, 47–8, 106, 114–5, 120
   distrust of 116–8, 134
Child rights *see also* human rights *and* United Nations Convention on the Rights of the Child 11, 16, 20, 22, 30, 37, 89–90, 96, 105–6, 118–9, 123–4, 126, 13
   debate 21
   critiques of 120–1
   to independent representation 17–8
   legal frameworks 38, 119–120, 122
   monitoring 15
   promotion and implementation of 19, 88
   right to education 16, 36, 86, 88, 89, 91
Citizenship 92, 116, 123

City, sense of belonging to 126, 128, 131
   children and young people as citizens 122
   education 37, 86
   student views on 126
   theory of 55–6
Community
   local communities 126–7, 132
Community cohesion 91, 92, 95
Confidentiality *see also* Anonymity, Ethics *and* Research methodologies
   limits to 32, 47
   in research context 30–2, 46
Consultation 116
   with students 36–9
Council of Europe 12, 14
Creative democracy, *see* Dewey, John
Curriculum 108, 112
   culturally inclusive 97, 98, 108
   national curriculum 94, 119
   strengthening Britishness 92
   student perspectives on 76, 78–80

Data collection 39–40, 45, 124, 126
Democracy
   American 128, 130
   as a British value 93
   democratic dialogue 56, 104
   democratic education 11–4, 38, 98
   democratic engagement 1, 119
   democratic ideas 133
   democratic participation 86, 107
   democratic practices in education 23, 116
   future of 105
   nation-states 95
   schools as democratic communities 14, 56
Dewey, John 11–2

Dialogue
    democratic dialogue *see* Democracy
    in research process 26
    student-teacher dialogue 36–9, 98
Diversity
    contexts of 12
    education for 86, 103–4, 108
    and global terrorism 95
    respect for 92, 100, 104
    in society 2
    of young people 14

Education *see also* Child rights
    for peace 86, 87, 88
    policy development 11, 75
    policy makers 19–20
Equality
    in discipline 103
    education to support 87, 100
    of rights 92
    as a shared value 93
    between students 13
    between students and teachers
        113
Ethics
    challenges 36
    of data collection 45
    in educational research 27, 42
    researching young people 2, 25–6,
        34, 50–1
Ethnic categorization 40–2, 48–9, 55
    self-reported 40–1, 55
Ethnicity *see also* ethnic categorization
    36, 41, 53, 55, 127
    stereotyping 81–2, 85
European Convention on Human
    Rights 17, 121
Extended learning, student
    perspectives of 69–70
Extra-curricular activities, student
    perspectives of 67–9

Facilities and equipment, student
    perspectives on 70–1
Faith schools 13, 87–9, 91, 99
Flexible school days, student
    perspectives on 61–3

'Gate-keepers' 42–3, 45–6
    negotiating with 45–6
Gender 36, 53, 55

Hill, John, MP 23–5
Human rights 15, 17, 100, 108, 112
    children's 1, 2, 37, 38, 39, 48, 53, 86,
        89, 135
    critiques of 120–2
    education 16, 98, 113
    of minority groups 56
    research 34
    universal 90

Identity
    and difference 93
    ethnic and cultural 41, 86, 88,
        127
    flexible 132
    individual 55
    national 95
    respect and recognition of 76,
        98
Immigration 5–9, 133
Inclusion 12–4, 89, 92, 98
Individual support, student
    perspectives on 71–2
Inequality 4, 19–20, 93, 95
Informed consent 30–1, 32, 42, 43,
    46–8
Islamophobia 93, 95

Killing Mockingbirds 3–9, 112, 133–5

Learning
    enjoyment of 76–8
    student perspectives on 84–5

McCrindle, Sir Robert, MP 23–5
Midlands (England) 35, 53, 54, 76
Multiculturalism 87, 92–6

Nation 2, 10, 126, 129–132, 133
    symbols of 128–9
National Children's Bureau (NCB) 25,
    27
    Guidelines on Research 30–4
National Union of School Students
    (NUSS) 23–6
National Union of Students (NUS)
    24–5
New technologies
    cyber bullying 102
    educational applications 70
    in research 42–5

Obama, Barack 15, 116–8
Office for Standards in Education
  (OFSTED) 48–9, 58
Orme (Baron), Stanley, MP 23–5

Parental rights 89–90
Participation (rights)
  of children and young people
    17–20, 21, 22, 26, 36–9, 42, 53,
    106, 109, 110, 113, 117, 119, 122,
    126, 135
  criticisms of 21
  in education 22, 98, 114
  exclusion from 107
Paternalism 118–9
Patriotism 95, 131–2
Phillips, Trevor 92–4
Physical education 67–8, 71
Power relations 26–34, 38, 47, 120
  in qualitative research 27

Racism 95, 100, 102, 103
Religious belief 96–9, 108
Religious education 69, 103–4
Representation 26, 29–30, 32–4
  in qualitative research 27
Research(ers) see also research
  methodologies 26–34, 35–52,
    135
  contexts of 26, 54–5
  impact upon subjects 30, 33–4
  incentives/rewards 30, 32–3
  responsibility of researchers to
    subjects 33–4
  values and principles 27–30, 32–4
  with young people 2, 26–7, 33, 47
Research methodologies 25, 39–52,
    123–6
  focus group interviews 125–6
  online discussion 42–5
  questionnaires 39–43
  workshops 45–52, 113, 123–6
Respect 80, 85, 96–101, 113–5
Rough Eagles project 3–9, 134
Rudduck, J. and D. McIntyre (2007)
    36–7, 55–6, 84, 116

Schools see also faith schools and
    democracy
  cleanliness and hygiene, student
    perspectives on 58–9, 66, 74

physical environment of, student
    perspectives on 53–4, 57–61, 74
  relationship with the wider
    community 69–70
  rules and discipline, student
    perspectives on 63–5
  security of, student perspectives on
    59, 66–7, 71
  young people's criticisms of 105
School uniform, student perspectives
    on 65–6
Special educational needs (SEN) 49, 91
Students see young people and children
Student behaviour, student
    perspectives on 82–3
Student councils 14, 64, 110–1, 113–4,
    116, 119
Supreme Court of Canada 90, 98

Teachers 57, 74, 115, 117, 126, 131,
    132, 135
  black and minority teachers 30, 32,
    68–9
  as 'gatekeepers' 45–7 see also
    'gate-keepers'
  as mentors 71–2
  conflict with students 64, 112
  dialogue with students 38, 98
  expertise of 107
  listening to students 114–6
  racism 103–4
  respect for students see also respect
    99–101, 114–5
  sexism 103
  teacher-student relationship 80–2,
    85, 97, 113
  teaching styles 76–9, 87, 119
Teaching, student perspectives on
    114–5
Thatcher, Lady Margaret, MP 23–5
To Kill a Mockingbird (Harper Lee) 3–9
Tolerance
  education for 86, 87, 88, 91, 92, 98,
    99, 104
  religious 90, 97, 104
Transparency 12–4

United Nations Committee on the
    Rights of the Child see also child
    rights 15–20, 21, 36, 37, 87, 119
  criticism of the UK 19–20, 36, 87

United Nations Convention on the
Rights of the Child (CRC) *see also*
child rights 14–20, 21–2, 25,
35–6, 37, 38, 39, 48, 86, 88, 91,
92, 106, 108–9, 112–3, 116,
119–122, 124, 126, 132, 133
article 2 116
article 3 106
article 5 106, 116
article 12 35–6, 38–9, 106, 109–110,
116, 122, 124, 126, 132, 133
article 13 106, 113
article 14 106
article 15
article 19 122
article 29 86, 88, 120
article 42 120
jurisprudence (UK) 17–20
obligations of schools/education
authorities 18–20

UK compliance/implementation
15–20
United States of America (USA) 2, 3–9,
15, 92–3, 119, 123–132, 133–5
Universal Declaration of Human
Rights (1948) 16, 126

Voice(s)
critiques of pupil voice 1, 26,
126
different 56
unheard 1
young people's and children's 21–2,
26, 39, 56, 110, 112

Young people *see also* children
pressure to succeed 79, 85
as researchers 29, 45–52, 49–52
as research subjects 2–3, 26–34,
35–52 *see also* research